I0294304

Writing Is Thinking

Writing Is Thinking

Strategies for All Content Areas

Edited by
Holly S. Atkins and Lin Carver

ROWMAN & LITTLEFIELD
Lanham • Boulder • New York • London

Published by Rowman & Littlefield
An imprint of The Rowman & Littlefield Publishing Group, Inc.
4501 Forbes Boulevard, Suite 200, Lanham, Maryland 20706
www.rowman.com

86-90 Paul Street, London EC2A 4NE, United Kingdom

British Library Cataloguing in Publication Information Available

Library of Congress Cataloging-in-Publication Data

Names: Atkins, Holly S., 1958- editor. | Carver, Lin, 1955- editor.
Title: Writing is thinking : strategies for all content areas /
Edited by Holly S. Atkins, Lin Carver.
Description: Lanham : Rowman & Littlefield, [2022] | Includes bibliographical references and index. | Summary: "Writing is Thinking examines the role writing plays in the transition from learning to write to writing to learn"—Provided by publisher.
Identifiers: LCCN 2021037522 (print) | LCCN 2021037523 (ebook) |
ISBN 9781475863239 (cloth) | ISBN 9781475863246 (paperback) |
ISBN 9781475863253 (epub)
Subjects: LCSH: English language—Composition and exercises—Study and teaching. |
Thought and thinking—Study and teaching. | Interdisciplinary approach in education.
Classification: LCC LB1576 .W744 2022 (print) | LCC LB1576 (ebook) |
DDC 428.0071—dc23/eng/20211006
LC record available at https://lccn.loc.gov/2021037522
LC ebook record available at https://lccn.loc.gov/2021037523

Dedication

This book is dedicated to our colleagues whose voices and expertise fill the pages of this text and to fellow educators who are making a difference in the lives of learners of all ages by teaching them to think, analyze, and write! We are grateful for your work here and for engaging your students in using the tool of writing as thinking each day.

Contents

Preface

In 2003, the National Commission on Writing for America's Families, Schools, and Colleges published a report on the state of writing instruction in American classrooms hailed as "groundbreaking." Titled *The Neglected "R": The Need for a Writing Revolution*, the commission's findings painted a grim picture of how the school reform movement of the previous twenty years had failed to include a focus on both the teaching and practice of writing. Nearly twenty additional years have passed since the report. How'd the revolution go, you ask? The most recent National Assessment of Educational Progress (2017), considered the nation's report card, found three-quarters of both twelfth and eighth graders lack proficiency in writing. Many hoped the Common Core State Standards, launched in 2009, would focus on writing largely ignored following the era of No Child Left Behind (2002), with the primary focus on reading comprehension assessed by standardized multiple-choice tests. Common Core Standards (2009) claimed writing was central to the curriculum by requiring students to demonstrate proficiency in essay writing—argumentative, informational, and narrative. The eight years between the large-scale rollout of Common Core State Standards or slightly modified individual state versions have not significantly improved students' writing proficiency measurements.

There have been and are bright spots. In 1974, James Gray and his University of California, Berkeley colleagues established what continues to be the gold standard in teacher professional development—The National Writing Project (NWP). Local writing project sites now reside on over 175 college campuses and engage over 2,500 K–12 educators in invitational summer institutes to grow as writers and teachers of writers. Three authors in this text have participated in a summer institute and served in leadership roles within a local NWP site. The tenets of NWP are naturally woven throughout their particular chapters and form the foundational core belief that connects this group of diverse educators. Writing matters.

Writing in the content area. Writing across the curriculum. Various terminology continues to be used to emphasize the need for all teachers to embrace writing in their discipline. An important but not new idea. As teachers, we've found ourselves leading school and district-based training urging the math, science, and social studies teachers to join us in supporting student writers. While some took up the cause, most often, we were met with expressions or overt statements communicating, "It's not my job to teach writing—it's yours."

What we propose in this text is a two-pronged perspective on writing. First, writing as a tool for learning. Learning math. Learning social studies. Learning science. The first two foundational chapters in the text emphasize this perspective. Learning to write in the early elementary school years becomes writing to learn as students progress through upper elementary, middle, high school, and college. Brain research supports the importance of this statement and the implications for writing as much more than the ability to craft an analytical essay. Writing has the potential to engage students in critical thinking, critical reflection. Second, the specific forms writing takes within disciplines. What writing is required of scientists, for example? How can science educators support students in the mastery of those forms?

CHAPTER COMPASS

A chapter compass may prove helpful to guide the reader in their journey of discovering writing as thinking and the content area strategies supporting this perspective. This compass leads the reader on a patterned path, a repeated structure. Each chapter begins with a brief activity designed to bring the reader into the focus of the chapter. Vignettes follow, in which the author(s) share experiences from their classrooms. The chapter continues with a consistent dual purpose of writing as thinking and specific strategies for classroom teachers to make this happen.

Does the book need to be read sequentially? Not necessarily, however, we do recommend you read chapters 1 and 2 first. These present foundational principles echoed throughout the remaining chapters. Subsequent chapters will prove more meaningful when read after these two chapters.

Chapter 3 asks the reader to consider the importance of bias-free language in writing and how writing becomes a tool for social change. In chapter 4, the authors' perspective is writing as a reflection or snapshot of thinking. Takeaways from this chapter include practical writing activities from multigenre projects to six-word memoirs.

Note-taking is ubiquitous throughout classrooms, and the authors of chapter 5 make a case for building on writing as thinking by engaging students in note-*making* instead of note-*taking*. Read and implement the tools suggested in this chapter. Your students will thank you!

In chapters 6–9, we turn the lens to writing in specific content areas: math, science, social studies, and English/language arts. Should readers focus only on their content area? No, not at all. Our belief in writing as thinking is a thread connecting each content area and each educator. Reading about writing to support science learning as a mathematics teacher will prove beneficial and highlight connections and tools to be used and adapted. Education should involve breaking down silos. There's no comfort or growth for you or your students staying within the confines of your discipline home.

We hope readers leave with the what, why, and how of writing and thinking.

Chapter 1

Writing-to-Learn

Lin Carver and Lauren Pantoja

Is writing just a concern of the English/Language Arts teacher or does it impact all teachers? What does writing-to-learn mean?

Before reading this chapter, think about the statements in the following anticipation guide. Decide if you agree or disagree with each statement. After reading the chapter revisit the statements in the anticipation guide and determine if you would still answer them in the same way.

ANTICIPATION GUIDE

1. Writing helps to clarify and expand thinking.
2. Writing-to-learn and learning to write are the same thing.
3. Students need to understand the writing process to write in the content area.
4. There is no difference in effectiveness whether notes are typed or handwritten.
5. Note-taking is the most important type of writing used in the content area.

VIGNETTE

A new family with two teen girls moved into the house across the street. I also had two teens at my house and the four became fast friends. It wasn't long into the school year when the oldest teen, Olivia, approached me indicating she was struggling in many of her classes. I asked her to describe her study habits. Olivia indicated that she took copious notes in class and read all of the required material. She truly felt she was giving it her best effort.

I explained to her that taking notes and doing the required reading were important learning activities, but she needed to think about what she was doing with the notes. My suggestion was,

> Take your notes and reorganize or revise the information either onto index cards or in a new format and add any relevant connections from the text you are reading. Each day read over your new notes for just a few minutes marking them up with new connections or new information that you make.

Just a few weeks later a beaming Olivia appeared at my door once again, this time to tell me she had aced her most recent exams. She thanked me profusely. Of course, my recommendations were just good practice. Note-taking can be a rote activity—the real learning comes when students process and organize the information they have collected.

WRITING IS THINKING

In all instruction, our goal is to get learners to think about the content. The act of writing helps learners clarify and communicate their thoughts. Theoreticians and practitioners have indicated that writing helps to promote critical thinking and learning (Applebee, 1985). Writing forces individuals to think critically about the ideas and to express them in a way that others will understand. When individuals write about their learning, it helps transform general ideas into specific concepts. Einstein (n.d.) stated, "If you can't explain it simply, you don't understand it well enough." As content educators, our goal is to take our learners to the point where they have mastered the content. So, the question we face is how do we use writing to teach or assess content mastery?

Research indicates that integrating writing in instruction enhances comprehension (Brandenburg, 2002). Writing about a topic "requires deeper processing than reading alone entails" (Fordham et al., 2002, p. 151). Writing-to-learn in the content area "extends thinking, deepens understanding, and energizes the meaning-making process" (Knipper & Duggan, 2006, p. 462).

ROLE OF WRITING IN LEARNING

"Reading is like breathing in; writing is like breathing out" (Allyn, 2018). Students learn content through reading, but not just reading. Students also learn through classroom discussion, presentations, hands-on activities, or other medias, such as videos or podcasts (Sedita, 2013) as well as writing about, reorganizing, and reflecting on these experiences. Writing is integral to learning. Writing tasks should be based on the learning experiences occurring during instruction. "Writing-to-learn means using writing tools to promote content learning; when students write, they think on paper" (Sedita, 2013, p. 2).

Writing is a tool that students can use to review knowledge, organize their thinking, and evaluate their content understanding. Writing-to-learn can help learners explore, process, and express what they have learned or are in the process of learning. Writing should be a process to help learners think for themselves rather than just summarize what others have said about a topic (Beers & Howell, 2005). Research has investigated the impact of writing-to-learn in various content areas with particular emphasis on the sciences. Researchers have reported positive support for its use with preservice teachers (Balgopal & Wallace, 2009), high school physics (Bulluck, 2006), and economics classes (Brewer & Jozefowicz, 2006). Klein et al. (2007) examined both knowledge building and transfer and found a higher level of posttest concept transfer when comparing the differences between writing and speaking. Fry and Villagomez (2012) determined that through writing-to-learn activities many students improved their metacognitive and reflective thinking. This was evidenced in deeper and richer writing responses to the prompts provided.

However, just including writing does not automatically enhance student learning. The research suggests that in order for writing to be effective, there are specific conditions to be met. Bangert-Drowns et al. (2004) conducted a meta-analysis of forty-eight writing-to-learn studies that were conducted on the K–12 level. They determined that writing-to-learn can have a small to medium effect size, but the effect size increased the longer students were exposed to writing-to-learn experiences that required metacognition.

To better understand the significance of this finding, it is important to have a general understanding of effect size. "Effect size is a quantitative measure of the magnitude of the experimental effect. The larger the effect size the stronger the relationship between two variables" (McLeod, 2019, para 2). Essentially, the effect size of writing-to-learn is more significant with time and the inclusion of metacognition, or the process of thinking about what they are learning. Students are metacognitive in their learning when they are aware of their learning and thinking or when they monitor and assess their understanding and performance (Chick, 2013). In their report, "The Neglected 'R': The Need for a Writing Revolution" the College Board stated, "Writing is not simply a way for students to demonstrate what they know. It is a way to help them understand what they know" (p. 13).

WRITING-TO-LEARN VERSUS LEARNING TO WRITE

Writing-to-learn and learning to write are two different activities (Fisher & Frey, 2004). Writing-to-learn in the content area is not about developing a piece of writing that will go through multiple changes and result in a polished, published document. In the content area, writing-to-learn should help to further meaning development and learning. Writing-to-learn should focus on creating active involvement in connecting and integrating ideas presented from the text or classroom instruction (Johnson et al., 1993). By incorporating writing-to-learn activities within the content area classroom, instructors can provide opportunities for students to recall, clarify, and question content information. It also helps learners to identify areas or topics where they have questions or concerns (Knipper & Duggan, 2006).

WRITING-TO-LEARN VERSUS WRITING TO COMMUNICATE

There are three major purposes in writing to communicate: writing to inform, instruct, or persuade. However, writing-to-learn is different. In writing-to-learn we write to objectify our content perceptions. The primary focus is not to communicate but to order and analyze our experiences and understanding. In this way, the written language creates the tool for discovering, shaping, and understanding (Fulwilern & Young, 1982).

Writing-to-learn enhances content mastery, but it also has additional positive effects. It does impact the writers' ability to communicate even though the initial goal was to increase their learning. Writing-to-learn helps students mature as more effective communicators (Parker & Goodkin, 1987).

CONTENT AREA WRITING ROPE

Scarborough's (2001) reading rope has been used for many years to represent the different components of the reading process. Each strand of the rope represents a separate skill that is combined with others to help create strong proficient readers. The reading rope is composed of both upper and lower strands. The word recognition strands of phonological awareness, decoding, and sight vocabulary work together to help create accurate, fluent, and increasingly automatic reading through repetition and practice, while at the same time the language comprehension strands of background knowledge, vocabulary, language structures, verbal reasoning, and literacy knowledge help to reinforce one another. The upper and the lower strands are woven together to produce a skilled reader. This skilled reading is developed through extended instruction and practice.

In the same way, writing is not a single skill that develops just in the language arts classroom. It too is composed of upper- and lower-level skills. Multiple versions of the writing rope have been created, but we have revised the rope to reflect how content area instruction can be used to support writing growth (see figure 1.1). The lower-level linguistic encoding process section of the rope tends to begin in the primary level classroom and continue to develop throughout the K–12 experience. These lower-level processes develop and increase in their automaticity, but they tend not to be addressed in secondary content instruction.

However, the higher-level thinking processes occur in a specific context so that informed writing can occur. Without this contextual basis, learners experience more difficulty processing or conveying knowledge. Content knowledge, content vocabulary, written discourse structure, critical thinking, and executive function provide the foundation for being able to write about the content.

Learners increase their content knowledge through exposure to texts, lectures, videos, and presentations about the content which typically occurs in the content area instruction. However, learners also bring their real-world experiences and prior knowledge into the instructional setting. This knowledge is expanded through teacher or student questioning. Questioning plays an integral part in learning by engaging students in the learning process and providing opportunities for inquiry. “It challenges levels of thinking and informs whether students are ready to progress with their learning. Questions

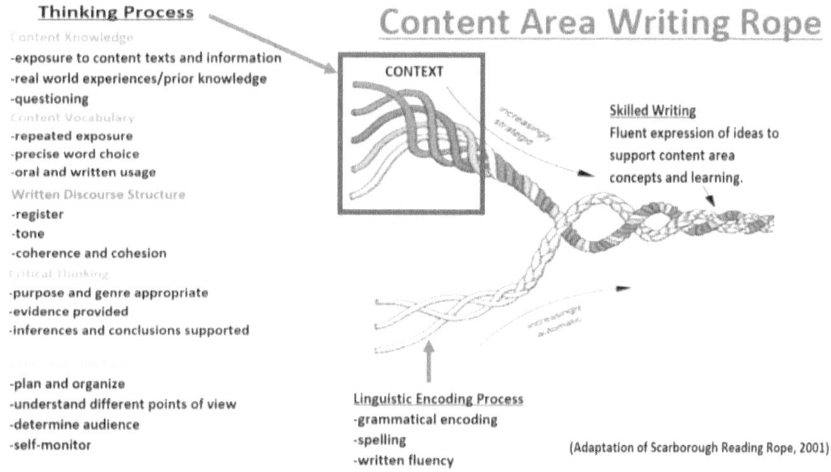

Figure 1.1 Content Area Writing Rope.

that probe for deeper meaning foster critical thinking skills and higher-order capabilities such as problem-solving" (Doherty, 2017, para. 1). Questioning also occurs metacognitively with self-talk to support understanding of learning. The process of questioning encourages the creation of critical thinkers who are able to express their ideas orally and in writing.

An understanding of specific content vocabulary is a necessary prerequisite for content area writing. Word learning is a difficult process requiring time and repeated exposures (Sinatra et al., 2011) through teacher modeling, guided, and independent practice. This repetition will help learners to be able to use the precise word choice needed to convey content area concepts. In science, writers need to know the names of specific tools such as beakers and test tubes, rather than referring to them as things or glass containers. Learners tend not to arrive in the content area classroom with an understanding of the content area vocabulary. Vocabulary instruction needs to focus on content area words as well as the meaning of prefixes, suffixes, and base and root words that are used in the specific content areas (Brooke, n.d.). Opportunities for both written and oral vocabulary usage are important components since oral usage often precedes written usage. Internalization of new vocabulary generally occurs once new words reach the level of being applied to the learner's writing.

Written discourse is composed of many elements. Register involves the learner's ability to determine the level at which the information should be shared: formal, informal, or neutral. Formal register is generally used for professional or business writing. The informal register is more conversational. The neutral register is nonemotional and focuses on factual information that would be used in technical writing. Formal registry tends to be more rule governed than either of the other two. Some of the rules that govern formal registry include writing in the third person, avoiding slang and idioms, and the use of longer more complex sentences (Really Learn English, n.d.). Tone encompasses the writer's attitude toward the reader and the subject. The tone that is used in the writing affects how the reader will interpret its message (Ober, 1985). Coherence and cohesion in writing refer to the way a text is organized so that it flows logically. Coherence refers to the way the elements within the text are linked together to make the text semantically meaningful. Lexical cohesion refers to the meaningful relationship between sentence elements. Grammatical cohesion is the relationship between the grammatical elements within the text (Rhalmi, 2021).

Critical thinking is an important element of the writing process because it brings together the three components already discussed. An understanding of the specific genre and purpose of the written text is required for critical thinking. Writers who have an understanding of genre and purpose will be better able to determine the appropriate structure, tone, and register needed for addressing the audience through their writing. When writers write they need to determine the appropriate genre for the written text based upon their particular goal which can be anything from telling a story, to arguing a position, to entertaining or explaining. All of these factors will impact the organization, rhetorical devices, and the linguistic features used within the written text (Dirgeyasa, 2015). Another important aspect of the critical thinking process when writing is finding evidence from sources used to support the thinking about the task or topic. Finding evidence that has a true, logical, and relevant connection to the task requires a discerning mind. Not all evidence is appropriate and without the right evidence, there will be little coherence or cohesion—important characteristics of the Written Discourse Structure strand. Even after drawing inferences and conclusions from the evidence mined from the texts, writers must provide support, elaboration, or commentary explaining how the evidence supports their thinking. Writing is a complex process that relies heavily on students' understanding of genre and purpose and their ability to make inferences and draw conclusions after deciphering evidence in support of a topic or task.

Executive function is the culminating strand in the thinking process. It focuses on the writer's ability to combine the other components into an organized project. It begins with writers' abilities to plan and organize the information to be conveyed. Writers need to understand various viewpoints on the topic to be discussed, their own and those of others. Writers need to determine who the audience will be and how to write for that particular audience. Throughout the process, writers need to self-monitor to ensure they are conveying their ideas fluently, accurately, and in an appropriate format.

The lower skills included in the content area writing rope encompass the linguistic encoding process. These are the skills taught during the learning to write phase of writing. These begin to be developed during the primary grades and become increasingly automatic as the learner matures. Grammatical encoding refers to the writer's understanding of the subject, verb, object agreement, and word order. This is further expanded to include the appropriate use of transition words and phrases (Psychology Concepts, 2020). Spelling skills develop as the learner masters the encoding words containing regular and irregular spelling patterns. Written fluency refers to the learner's ability to write with a "natural flow and rhythm. Fluent writers use grade-appropriate word patterns, vocabulary, and content" (Campos, 2020, para. 1).

HANDWRITING VERSUS TECHNOLOGY

Much importance has been placed on note-taking because of its improved learning and support for preparation for exams. The encoding function of note-taking focuses on improving students' retention of content information without studying it. Its storage function refers to whether note-taking during class helps students learn the concepts while studying (DiVesta & Gray, 1972).

In a well-publicized study, Mueller and Oppenheimer (2014) compared the effectiveness of handwritten notes to those produced on a laptop. During their study, college students watched five videos and took notes either longhand or by typing notes on a laptop keyboard. A test that included both factual and conceptual questions was then administered. The researchers found that performance between the two groups on factual questions did not differ; however, performance on questions related to concepts was significantly greater for those who took notes longhand (Mueller & Oppenheimer, 2014). Examination of the notes revealed that typed notes tended to reflect a transcription of the lecture, but they did not reveal deep processing of the content. The word count and the verbatim overlap between the lecture content and the notes were greater for those notes taken on a laptop.

Morehead et al. (2019) further investigated this issue by comparing the use of e-writers which are digital devices but use a stylus rather than typing function, laptops, and longhand note-taking. A variety of e-writers exist, but an e-writer is a device that can be used to jot down notes by writing on the digital screen itself using a stylus or your finger (Strickland, 2012). Moorehead et al.'s findings indicated that note-taking of students who used e-writers most closely paralleled outcomes from those taking notes by longhand on paper. Students who used e-writers tended to perform as well as those who took notes using other methods based on word count, verbatim overlap, test relevance, and the number of ideas included in the notes. Although research continues to develop, note-taking using e-writers seems to involve similar processes and conceptual retention as taking notes on paper. Although further research is needed to more fully evaluate the use of e-writers as effective note-taking devices, the preliminary evidence seems to indicate that they are as effective as longhand note-taking (Morehead et al., 2019).

WRITING-TO-LEARN STRATEGIES

Note-taking is an activity often identified when discussing writing-to-learn, but it is certainly not the only one. A variety of writing activities can be implemented in the content area classroom. Some examples are listed below. Writing-to-learn activities tend to be short, informal writing tasks whose purpose is to help students think through key content concepts or ideas. It is important that these activities require little class time so as not to distract from content instruction. Their goal is content synthesis and comprehension.

These activities are not just copying or filling in blanks since research suggests this has limited learning value. Content mastery is increased when students are at the center of their own learning. This enables them to master content and to improve their skill at expressing ideas while investigating connections, discerning processes, raising questions, and discovering solutions.

Focused Freewriting

Focused freewriting simply means writing whatever comes into your head related to a specific topic or concept. This can be particularly useful at the beginning of a class or the beginning of a topic to immediately engage learners because there are no wrong answers. Sharing after the activity might increase participation as well. Typically, this activity is limited to a specific length of time (Richmond Education, n.d.b.).

Entry Slips and Exit Slips

Entry or exit slips are a short 5-minute activity that can be used at either the beginning or the end of class, as their name indicates. Learners are asked to respond in writing to a question posed by the instructor. The responses help the instructor to gauge students' understanding of the information presented previously so that instruction can be appropriately focused (Richmond Education, n.d.a.).

Reader-Response Writing

As content area instructors, sometimes just knowing what someone else says about a topic is not enough. Learners need to be able to analyze the author's bias as well as their own bias about a topic. The reader-response writing activity is an effective choice for helping students understand bias. Learners divide a paper in half down the middle. On the left-hand side, the student records the author's bias, and on the right-hand side the student records his own bias (see table 1.1). Listing the biases forces the students to think critically about what they are reading while recording their own helps them to see similarities or differences (Richmond Education, n.d.c.).

Table 1.1 Reader-Response Writing

The Author's Bias	*My Bias*

Sentence/Passage Springboard

Not all sentences we read or hear have the same impact. Some sentences shock or surprise us, while others may inspire or uplift us. Students are asked to respond in writing to a particular sentence or passage that was shared orally or through content readings (Richmond Education, n.d.d.).

Student-Formulated Questions

Often during instruction, questions are asked by the instructor. Asking students to write down how and why questions about the topic before it is discussed can be an effective way to increase student involvement and engagement. This process helps students better understand the content and determine the relevance of the topic to themselves and the world around them (Richmond Education, n.d.f.).

The Short Summary

Summarizing information that is read or presented in a class lecture is challenging for some students. This can be even more of a challenge when students are limited to a certain amount of words. Limiting this to 15–50 words (depending on the amount of content covered) helps them to focus on the most important points and helps to improve comprehension, but its brief format is not threatening (Richmond Education, n.d.e.).

Dialectical or Double-Entry Journals

The major difference between dialectical or double-entry journals and typical journals is evidenced by the vertical line drawn down the center of the page dividing it into two portions. Each portion has a different function. The Dialectic Reaction Journal could be set up so that the left side is used to record important points and the right side is used to list additional questions the student still has or personal observations related to the facts in the left-hand column (see table 1.2). In the Evidence-Based Answer Journal format, the left-hand column is used to record important questions students should be able to answer about the content and the

Table 1.2 Dialectic Reaction Journal

Important Fact	*Personal Reaction or Additional Comments*

Table 1.3 Evidence-Based Answer Journal

Question	*Answer and Its Location in the Text*

right-hand column can be used to record an evidence-based answer and where the answer is located within the text (see table 1.3) (Richmond Education, n.d.g.).

Focused Note-Taking

Focused note-taking is an AVID strategy that supports note-taking as a process. The AVID note-taking process involves a five-step process.

- Creating Notes—selecting, paraphrasing, arranging information
- Processing Notes—highlighting, adding information, deleting information
- Connecting Thinking—asking questions, identifying points of confusion
- Summarizing and Reflecting on Learning—crafting a summary of the most important information
- Applying Learning—using notes as a resource for assignments or activities (McKinney et al., 2018, p. 98).

Students compare notes with partners throughout the note-taking process and make necessary adjustments (McKinney et al., 2018). Students can discuss one another's questions and wonderings to deepen their thinking about the notes they take (McKinney et al., 2018). Focused note-taking helps students organize and deepen their learning.

Peer Feedback

Peer feedback is an opportunity for students to put a critique in writing with a personal audience in mind. It is more complex than simply finding errors in a peer's work. It should focus on clarity and idea development in a reflective, not a corrective way (Gardner, 2019). Feedback should be

- specific—related directly to the ideas and verbiage of the text,
- prescriptive—aimed at improving the work,
- actionable—steps leading to improvement described,
- kind—phrased using thoughtful word choice that encourages the writer (Gardner, 2019).

When students analyze and reflect on the work of others, they take their own learning to a higher level.

CONCLUSION

It is impossible to write without thinking! People can copy words or definitions from a dictionary without thinking, but writing informatively, argumentatively, instructionally, descriptively, or creatively requires thought. If we want students to reflect, solidify, or extend their learning, writing is a step in the right direction and supports this process.

Refer back to the anticipation guide at the beginning of this chapter; consider if your thinking about each of the statements has been affirmed or changed.

1. Writing helps to clarify and expand thinking.

   Yes, writing does a lot more, but if there is confusion, putting their thinking or learning into words helps the learners retain and clarify what they have learned. Often when we write, connections are made, expanding thinking.
2. Writing-to-learn and learning to write are the same thing.

   Not necessarily. When we are learning to write, we are learning about the writing process, but many writing strategies support new content learning.
3. Students need to understand the writing process to write in the content area.

   Maybe. The writing process involves prewriting, drafting, revising, editing, and publishing, and although you might not use the process itself when writing in the content area using the writing process is not limited to English classes.
4. There is no difference in effectiveness whether notes are typed or handwritten.

   Typed notes tend to reflect more of a transcription of a lecture whereas when Mueller and Oppenheimer (2014) compared handwritten and typed notes, they found that performance on questions related to concepts was significantly greater for those who took notes longhand. When notes taken on an e-writer were compared, there did not seem to be a difference in the quality of the notes between the digitally transcribed notes and those that were handwritten.
5. Note-taking is the most important type of writing used in the content area.

   Note-taking is important, but only if it involves thinking! Note-taking as a process is very powerful; however, there are many additional writing activities that support learning in the content classroom.

Writing is a complex process, but the more we write the better we become not just as writers but as learners and thinkers.

REFERENCES

Albert Einstein Quotes. (n.d.). BrainyQuote.com. https://www.brainyquote.com/quotes/albert_einstein_383803.

Allyn, P. (2018). Reading is like breathing in; Writing is like breathing out. *Scholastic EDU.* https://edublog.scholastic.com/post/reading-breathing-writing-breathing-out.

Applebee, A. N. (1985). Writing and reasoning. *Review of Educational Research, 54*(4), 577–596.

Balgopal, M. M., & Wallace, A. M. (2009). Decisions and dilemmas: Using writing-to-learn activities to increase ecological literacy. *Journal of Environmental Education, 40*(3), 13–26.

Bangert-Drowns, R. L., Hurley, M. M., & Wilkinson, B. (2004). The effects of school-based writing-to-learn interventions on academic achievement: A meta-analysis. *Review of Educational Research, 74*, 29–58.

Beers, S., & Howell, L. (2005). Using writing-to-learn across the content areas: An ASCD action tool. http://www.ascd.org/ASCD/pdf/books/beersAT2005b_sample_pages.pdf.

Brandenburg, M. L. (2002). Advanced math? Write! *Educational Leadership, 30*(3), 67–68.

Brewer, S. M., & Jozefowicz, J. J. (2006). Making economic principles personal: Student journals and reflection papers. *Journal of Economic Education, 37*(2), 202–216.

Brooke, E. (n.d.). The critical role of oral language in reading instruction and assessment. Lexia. https://www.lexialearning.com/resources/white-papers/oral-language.

Bullock, S. (2006). Building concepts through writing-to-learn in college physics classrooms. *Ontario Action Researcher, 9*(2), 1–8.

Campos, J. M. (2020). Seven effective strategies to build writing fluency. English Post. https://englishpost.org/strategies-build-writing-fluency/#:~:text=Writing%20Fluency%20refers%20to%20a,variety%20of%20writing%20improvement%20activities.

Chick, N. (2013). Metacognition. Vanderbilt University Center for Teaching. https://cft.vanderbilt.edu/guides-sub-pages/metacognition/.

Di Vesta, F. J., & Gray, G. S. (1972). Listening and note taking. *Journal of Educational Psychology, 63*, 8–14. https://doi.org/10.1037/h0032243.

Dirgeyasa, I., (2016). Genre-based approach: What and how to teach and to learn writing. *English Language Teaching, 9*, 45–51. http://dx.doi.org/10.5539/elt.v9n9p45.

Doherty, J. (2017). Skillful questioning: The beating heart of good pedagogy. https://impact.chartered.college/article/doherty-skilful-questioning-beating-heart-pedagogy/#:~:text=The%20issue%20that%20teachers%20face&text=Questioning%20serves%20many%20purposes%3A%20it,to%20progress%20with%20their%20learning.

Fordham, N. W., Wellman, D., & Sandman, A. (2002). Taming the text: Engaging and supporting students in social studies readings. *The Social Studies, 93*(4), 149–158.

Fry, S. W., & Villagomez, A. (2012). Writing-to-learn: Benefits and limitations. *College Teaching, 60*, 170–175.

Fulwiler, T., & Young, A. (1982). Introduction. In T. Fulwiler & A. Young (Eds.), *Language connections: Writing and reading across the curriculum* (pp. ix–xiii). National Council of Teachers of English.

Gardner, M. (2019). Teaching students to give peer feedback. *Edutopia*. https://www.edutopia.org/article/teaching-students-give-peer-feedback.

Johnson, J., Holcombe, M., Simms, G., & Wilson, D. (1993). Writing-to-learn in a content area. *The Clearing House, 66*(3), 155–158.

Klein, P. D., Piacente-Cimini, S., & Williams, L. A. (2007). The role of writing in learning from analogies. *Learning and Instruction, 17*(6), 595–611.

Knipper, K. J., & Duggan, T. J. (2006). Writing-to-learn across the curriculum: Tools for comprehension in content area classes. *The Reading Teacher, 59*(5), 462–470.

McLeod, S. (2019). What does effect size tell you? *Simply Psychology*. https://www.simplypsychology.org/effect-size.html#:~:text=Effect%20size%20is%20a%20quantitative,how%20substantially%20different%20they%20are.

McKinney, C., Glazebrook, B., Sanders, J., & Shapiro, D. (2018). *AVID writing for disciplinary literacy: A schoolwide approach*. AVID.

Morehead, K., Dunlosky, J., & Rawson, K. A. (2019). How much mightier is the pen than the keyboard for note-taking? A replication and extension of Mueller and Oppenheimer, *Educational Psychology Review, 31*, 753–780. https://doi.org/10.1007/s10648-019-09468-2.

Mueller, P. A., & Oppenheimer, D. M. (2014). The pen is mightier than the keyboard: Advantages of longhand over laptop note-taking. *Psychological Science, 25*, 1159–1168. https://doi.org/10.1177/0956797614524581.

Ober, S. (1995). *Contemporary business communication* (2nd ed.). Houghton Mifflin.

Parker, R. P., & Goodkin, V. (1987). *The consequences of writing: Enhancing learning in the disciplines*. Boynton/Cook.

Psychology Concepts. (2020). Linguistic encoding. http://www.psychologyconcepts.com/linguistic-encoding/.

Rhalmi, M. (2021). The difference between coherence and cohesion. https://www.myenglishpages.com/blog/difference-between-coherence-and-cohesion/.

Really Learn English. (n.d.). Learn English vocabulary and easy English grammar. https://www.really-learn-english.com/.

Richmond Education. (n.d.a). Writing across the curriculum: Entry and exit slips. http://writing2.richmond.edu/wac/entrexit.html.

Richmond Education. (n.d.b). Writing across the curriculum: Freewrite. http://writing2.richmond.edu/wac/freewrit.html.

Richmond Education. (n.d.c). Writing across the curriculum: Reader response. http://writing2.richmond.edu/wac/r_respon.html.

Richmond Education. (n.d.d). Writing across the curriculum: Sentence/passage springboard. http://writing2.richmond.edu/wac/sprngbrd.html.

Richmond Education. (n.d.e.). Writing across the curriculum: Short summary. http://writing2.richmond.edu/wac/summary.html.
Richmond Education. (n.d.f.). Writing across the curriculum: Student-formulated questions. http://writing2.richmond.edu/wac/studqust.html.
Richmond Education. (n.d.g.). Writing across the curriculum: Student-formulated questions. http://writing2.richmond.edu/wac/2entrynb.html.
Scarborough, H. S. (2001). Connecting early language and literacy to later reading (dis)abilities: Evidence, theory, and practice. In S. Neuman & D. Dickson (Eds.), *Handbook for research in early literacy* (pp. 97–110). Guilford Press.
Sedita, J. (2013). Learning to write and writing-to-learn. In M. C. Hougen (Ed.), *Fundamentals of literacy instruction and assessment:* 6-12, (pp. 97–114). Paul H. Brookes. https://keystoliteracy.com/wp-content/uploads/2012/08/Learning%20to%20Write%20and%20Writing%20to%20Learn.pdf.
Sinatra, R., Zygouris-Coe, V., & Dasinger, S. (2011). Preventing a vocabulary lag: What lessons are learned from research. *Reading & Writing Quarterly, 28*(4), 333–357.
Strickland, J. (2012, April). How e-writers work. https://electronics.howstuffworks.com/gadgets/otehr-gadgets/e-writers.htm.
The College Board. (2003). The report of the National Commission on Writing in America's schools and colleges. *The Neglected "R": The need for a writing revolution.* https://archive.nwp.org/cs/public/print/resource/2432.

Chapter 2

Writing with the Brain in Mind

Candace Roberts

TO BEGIN . . .

Think of a piece of writing that is memorable to you. It may be something for a school assignment. Perhaps it is a letter, an editorial, a blog. Maybe it is a type of personal writing, a poem, a story, or a eulogy for a loved one. Once you've selected the piece, engage in a "quick write" about it. Write down the title or topic and the type of writing it was. Write down three reasons why you remember and/or chose this piece of writing. At the end of this chapter, we'll discuss why what you wrote matters.

Educators persistently search for effective ways to facilitate meaningful and lasting learning. Instructional practices often draw from various disciplines, including psychology, sociology, biology, and educational research and theory. Perhaps the most powerful field has emerged in the past two decades—the field of neuroscience. We now know more about how the brain functions and how it best learns, so we can make pedagogical decisions that create the most effective learning experiences. Most importantly, for our purposes in this book, writing has emerged as a teaching tool with a formidable impact on student learning. Dr. Judy Willis, a board-certified neurologist for over fifteen years and a classroom teacher for ten years, explained that

> the practice of writing can enhance the brain's intake, processing, retaining, and retrieving of information. Through writing, students can increase their comfort with and success in understanding complex material, unfamiliar concepts, and subject-specific vocabulary. When writing is embedded throughout the curriculum, it promotes the brain's attentive focus to classwork and homework, boosts long-term memory, illuminates patterns, gives the brain time for reflection, and

> when well-guided, is a source of conceptual development and stimulus of the brain's highest cognition. (Willis, 2011c, para. 3)

While the use of writing in classrooms has gone on largely unchanged for decades, if not centuries, this chapter will show how the integration of cognitive science and writing pedagogy can bring about the most powerful content learning.

NEUROSCIENCE: WHAT TEACHERS NEED TO KNOW

Thanks to the development of positive emission tomography (PET scans) in the late 1980s and functional magnetic resonance imaging (fMRI) in the 1990s, scientists have been able to look into the brain, map its structures, and observe the brain in action. We can now watch as learning happens. The brain was once thought to be static and unchangeable; what you're born with is what you have. Today we know that the brain is changing all the time, even into later life. Neuroplasticity is the brain's ability to constantly make new connections and change how it is wired. Every time you learn something new, you change the brain (Brown et al., 2014; Jensen, 2008; Scalise & Field, 2017). Learning occurs when neurons connect to one another through branchlike extensions called dendrites. Connections between neurons organize themselves and form pathways that thicken as they are used or accessed more frequently. The more connections that are established, the stronger the memory. Like a path in the woods, the more these pathways are traveled (accessed), the thicker and more easily accessible they become. This makes memories stronger, and more importantly, when a brain is confronted with a new problem, pathways that have been accessed before can be accessed and connected to construct new ideas, to think critically, and to solve problems. The human brain has over 100 billion neurons, but it's not the individual neurons that make us smart, it's the connections that do (Jensen, 2008).

Because of neuroplasticity, "teachers are not simply teaching a curriculum . . . they play an instrumental role in shaping and changing the brain" (Scalise & Felde, 2017, p. 11). This should be a statement of responsibility as well as empowerment for teachers. "Every student in your class has the capacity for change" (Jensen, 2005, p. 13). As John Hattie (2012) explained, "We must consider ourselves positive change agents for the students who come to us. . . . Teachers' beliefs and commitments are the greatest influence on student achievement over which we can have some control" (p. 25).

So if we're in the business of changing the brain, we must understand how the brain changes. The brain is made up of four lobes: (1) occipital lobe (middle-back, responsible for vision); (2) temporal lobes (around/above ears, responsible for hearing, memory, language); (3) parietal lobe (top/back of head, responsible for processing higher sensory and language functions); and (4) frontal lobe (around the forehead, includes prefrontal cortex, involved in judgment, problem-solving, planning, creativity, short-term memory). Because of the fundamental nature of connections, the more areas of the brain that are activated during meaning-making, the more opportunities there are for neural pathways to be established and the more lasting the learning. Connectivity is the critical quality of the brain, not its individual structures (Jensen, 2005, p. 10). When the brain takes in new information, multiple structures are activated. Within the temporal lobe is the hippocampus, whose primary function involves human learning and memory. There, short-term memories are turned into long-term memories which are then stored in various other and often multiple areas of the brain. Also within the temporal lobe is the amygdala. This is often referred to as the switching station of the brain because it is responsible for our fight, flight, or freeze response to threatening situations. If a human (or in our case, student) experiences a threat or stress, such as fear, anxiety, anger, humiliation, or aggression, the amygdala responds as if it were a physical threat and sends out messages to the brain to emit stress hormones (cortisol and adrenaline) to equip the body to address the threat. This works well as a survival mechanism, but not so much in a classroom (or office, or home) because it prevents the prefrontal cortex from doing its job—thinking. When under threat or stress, the amygdala diverts the brain's energy and processing away from the prefrontal cortex (responsible for executive functioning, including working memory, organizing, self-regulation, decision-making, planning, and critical thinking) and from the hippocampus (responsible for turning short-term memory into long-term memory). Again, great for survival, but it has significant implications for learning if students are experiencing stress. Knowing this information not only helps us understand obstacles our students may be facing because of stress-induced outside-of-school, but it also informs how we plan our assignments and assessments, and most importantly, how we create a classroom community that reduces stress and feels safe and supportive.

PRINCIPLES OF BRAIN-BASED LEARNING

Understanding what the brain needs and how it learns provides powerful information that can help teachers to make more effective instructional decisions by aligning how they teach with how the brain works. The following are some key principles of brain learning that will lead to effective pedagogical approaches and support the use of specific writing strategies discussed later in this chapter.

- The brain is wired to search for meaning. Relevance matters.
- Memory is not stored in one location in the brain. Teaching that incorporates multiple modalities creates multiple pathways and is more effective in helping students create memories.
- The big picture can't be separated from the details.
- People learn best when solving realistic problems.
- Emotions play a significant part in memory. They can positively or negatively influence memory formation.
- Feedback is a learning strategy. Getting and applying feedback is how the brain learns, adapts, creates, and maintains memories that can be transferred to new challenges.

WRITING IS A MEANING-MAKING PROCESS

When students write about content, they must actively engage in discipline-based meaning-making by recognizing patterns, connecting to prior knowledge, and articulating understanding in their own words. Writing engages the prefrontal cortex (executive function) and activates older pathways to connect new information to what is already known. It can connect information from many sources, including lecture, reading, discussion, and collaboration (Willis, 2011c). Vygotsky described the cognitive dynamic that happens during the act of writing, explaining that the writer must engage in "deliberate semantics" in order to create a "web of meaning" (Vygotsky & Kozulin, 1986, p. 182). Emig (1977) asserted that "writing is integrative in perhaps the most basic possible sense. . . . Writing involves the fullest possible functioning of the brain, which entails the active participation in the process of both the left and right hemispheres" (p. 125). During the past two decades of research in cognitive science, the work of Vygotsky and Emig has been confirmed through PET and fMRI scans which show the many areas of the brain that are activated when someone writes, creating neural networks for connecting prior knowledge, meaning-making, metacognition, and memory-making. In her article, "The Brain-Based Benefits of Writing for Math and Science Learning" (2011c), neurologist and teacher, Judy Willis wrote:

> Writing can help the brain to develop the logical functions required for successful math and science learning. . . . When writing is incorporated in learning and assessment, there is increased opportunity to produce the ideal situation for active, attentive learning with collaboration, revision, and metacognition through personalization, and creativity. They are more likely to apply the effort, collaborate successfully, ask questions, revise work, and review foundational knowledge.

In its search for meaning, the brain thrives on relevance.

> Relevance is a function of the brain in making a connection from existing neural sites. . . . Relevance actually happens on a cellular level. An existing neuron simply connects with a nearby neuron to make a connection. If the content is irrelevant (lacks understanding or emotional valence), It's unlikely that a connection will be made. . . . The greater the number of links and associations that your brain creates, the more firmly the information is woven in neurologically. (Jensen, 2008, p. 180)

"If the brain does not ascertain meaning from the new information, it will drop it" (Sprenger, 2010, p. 31). Designing writing tasks that require students to make connections to their own lives or solve realistic problems will enhance relevance in any content area and support meaning-making, which in turn, makes memories possible. "You cannot recall information that your brain does not retain" (Sousa, 2017, p. 48).

MAKING MEMORIES

When a student writes, the brain engages in processing new information, searches for and creates new patterns, and develops neural pathways or "conceptual memory networks" (Willis, 2011c). As the writer assimilates, analyzes, integrates information, reaches conclusions, forms opinions, and articulates these complex concepts, they construct neural networks necessary for memory. Bundles of neurons link and bind together when they are used together. Neuroscientists often say "what fires together wires together." The more this is repeated (the more times connected information is accessed together), the thicker the networks become, and the easier it is to retrieve information to form new concepts or conclusions. This is the embodiment of neuroplasticity, the changing of the brain, and this is what teachers can orchestrate with appropriate strategies. Willis (2011c) explains that when students write in the content areas, the brain

> transforms formulas, procedures, graphs, and statistical analyses into words represent[ing] the brain's recognition of patterns . . . the facts, procedures, and observations are processed symbolically in the writing process—giving the memory another storage modality. . . . Writing is Memory Cement. (Willis, 2011c)

This process of meaning and memory-making is more important than the product or individual facts.

Scalise and Felde (2017) referred to writing as "a type of augmented memory system" for the brain (p. 266). The act of composing brings content information into focus, forces the brain to pay attention, and supports getting information into long-term memory. Just as the writing rope introduced in chapter 1 affirmed that writing is not a single skill, it is also not a singular cognitive process. It requires "content knowledge, content vocabulary, written discourse structure, critical thinking, and executive function" (Carver & Pantoja, 2022). This assemblage of complex cognitive actions forces the writer to engage in active and effortful cognition. Brown et al. (2014) explained that "learning is deeper and more durable when it's effortful" (p. 3). Bjork (1994) referred to this as engaging in "desirable difficulties," which trigger neural connections, prompt retrieval, and create neural networks, all supporting long-term memory and transfer. Nevertheless, for all of its myriad benefits, there is one significant caveat to introducing writing tasks—the unintended creation of cognitive overload. Cognitive overload occurs when the information processing demands on the brain exceed the ability of the brain to manage (Sweller, 1988). Sprenger (2010) explained that "cognitive overload, sensory overload, or short-term memory overload are all the same phenomenon: in a space that is meant for 5–7 bits of information, the 8th is either not going in or it's pushing another bit out" (p. 113). Jensen (2005) explained it as "too much, too fast, it won't last."

Cognitive overload not only occurs when a student is trying to juggle too much new information, but it can also occur when students are asked to engage in tasks requiring skills they have not yet mastered. In the content area classroom, this often happens when a teacher requires students to write a complete essay before students have mastered all the necessary component skills. Writers must juggle writing considerations such as voice, audience, main ideas, supporting details, organization, word choice, sentence fluency, conventions, and grammar. They must consider traditional structures such as introductions, topic sentences, paragraphing, and conclusions. They might need to consider the conventions of particular genres or literary devices such as style, tone, figurative language, and theme. They will have to consider the process of writing including brainstorming, drafting, revising, and editing, and they have to consider content—the information or message being conveyed. This presents cognitive overload for many good writers who have attained a certain level of proficiency with many of these skills. "Novices, on the other hand, have not achieved the same degree of fluency and automaticity in each of the component skills, and thus they struggle to combine skills that experts combine with relative ease and efficiency" (Ambrose et al., 2010, p. 105). As experts, many teachers do not fully grasp the cognitive constraints these demands cause writers and so do not use methods to scaffold and manage the resulting cognitive overload. Challenges that are too difficult can lead to frustration and hopelessness (Scalise & Felde, 2017). "To develop mastery, students must acquire component skills, practice integrating them, and know when to apply what they have learned" (Ambrose et al., 2010, p. 95). In order to reduce cognitive load, it is incumbent upon the teacher to focus on only a few skills or goals at a time. For content area teachers, expecting students to demonstrate proficiency in both writing and the new content may cause overload. Instead, focusing on the content would be the most important consideration in using writing as a tool for learning. Of the many writing activities that support critical thinking and memory-making in the content area without the expectation of mastery in writing skills, the following will be explored later in this chapter: summarizing, paraphrasing, describing, explaining, storytelling, data analysis, reflective writing, journaling, blogging, collaborating, revising, quick writes, freewriting, and graphic organizers.

EMOTIONS MATTER

For good and for bad, emotions have a decisive impact on learning (Brown et al., 2014; Jensen, 2008; Medina, 2012; Scadden, 2016; Scalise & Felde, 2017; Sousa, 2016, 2017; Whitman & Kelleher, 2016). As a survival mechanism, emotions take first priority over attention, processing, and memory formation, and yet we rarely consider the pedagogical implications of our students' emotional states. This chapter has already established the biological response to stress and fear when the amygdala acts as a switching station and diverts energy from executive functions to fight, flight, or freeze responses. With this information, teachers can intentionally work to reduce fear, anxiety, stress, and frustration, because reducing stress will increase learning (Sprenger, 2010). Just as important as reducing or eliminating negative emotions, teachers can capitalize on the cognitive impact of positive emotions.

While negative emotions can obstruct learning, positive emotions support it. "Good learning does not avoid emotions; it embraces them" (Jensen, 2005, p. 72). Positive emotions prompt the brain to produce neurotransmitters, specifically dopamine and serotonin, which enhance synaptic transmission—the chemical reaction when one neuron binds to another. These neurotransmitters are critical in creating neural pathways and memory formation. Jensen (2005) refers to these neurotransmitters as "memory fixative." Neurotransmitters are more likely to be produced when students perceive learning tasks to be engaging, relevant, attainable, and/or rewarding. Emotions can be intentionally aroused before or during a learning experience to embed memory (Jensen, 2005; Medina, 2014). When students experience positive emotions during learning, they are more likely "to make better perceptual maps . . . [and] are better able to sort out experiences and recall with more clarity"

(Jensen, 2008, p. 181). Simply stated, "whenever teachers can tie emotions to curriculum content, students are more likely to remember it" (Sousa, 2016, p. 55). Connecting emotions to content can happen via anticipation guides, reflective writing, current event connections, storytelling, or inviting students to make personal connections.

Providing choice can also be a determining factor in how students feel about their learning tasks (Scaddan, 2016; Scalise & Felde, 2017; Sousa, 2016; Sprenger, 2010). "Choice is a critical ingredient in maintain learning motivation. It literally alters the chemistry in the brain by lowering stress levels. Increasing positive feelings about the task promotes the production of dopamine and serotonin, two powerful neurotransmitters" (Scaddan, 2016, p. 13). Choice provides students with a sense of control and self-determination and is often part of a classroom climate that is student centered. Positive classroom climates promote respect and positive relationships among students. Hattie (2012) noted in his meta-analysis of more than 900 research studies examining more than 150 factors that influence learning, that classroom climate was among the most critical. He wrote that

> a positive, caring, respectful climate in the classroom is a prior condition to learning. Without students' sense that there is a reasonable degree of "control," sense of safety to learn, and sense of respect and fairness that learning is going to take place, there is little chance that much positive is going to occur. (p. 78)

Teachers who make intentional decisions about their students' emotional well-being also support their cognitive well-being. Since emotions have priority in the brain, by addressing affective variables such as relevance, confidence, safety, respect, belonging, and connection, teachers are doing exactly what the brain craves. Given that how students feel has a direct link to how they learn, emotions and classroom climate turn out to be the principal determining factors in student success.

FEEDBACK CHANGES THE BRAIN

Feedback is a powerful teaching strategy that can either increase or decrease emotions and student performance. Feedback has three concrete benefits: (1) it reduces stress, (2) it guides learning, and (3) it supports memory. Feedback, specifically formative feedback, reduces stress by helping students know if they are on target (Hattie, 2012; Jensen, 2008; Scalise & Felde, 2017). Formative assessment is designed to give students guidance and direction *during* the learning activity while there is still time to make adjustments. The stakes are lower and students know that with guidance, they can improve and meet expectations. Feedback that is only given at the end is summative and leaves little to no opportunity for correction or improvement on a learning activity. Regardless of whether the feedback is formative or summative, words of praise or criticism have a direct effect on students' emotions. "The feedback must be corrective and positive enough to tell the student what the desired change must be" (Jensen, 2005, p. 55). The teacher is in "a very powerful position of influence. . . . Emotions alter brain chemistry and neuronal data processing. It is important to use that power wisely" (Willis, 2011a, p. 97). We can discourage, overwhelm, or even crush spirits, or we can build up learners while providing guidance and opportunity for improvement.

Feedback guides learning (Ambrose et al., 2010; Bransford et al., 2000; Hattie, 2012; Scalise & Felde, 2017; Sousa, 2016; Sprenger, 2010). The brain is a pattern-seeking organ that "regulates learning process through feedback" (Scalise & Felde, 2017, p. 208). Hattie (2012) identified feedback as the third most impactful classroom variable (out of 150) influencing student achievement. Sousa (2016) reported that "immediate specific feedback is one of the most powerful factors for increasing student achievement" (p. 68). Scalise and Felde explained that

> feedback ***is*** instruction. . . . [It] supports the learner's ability to regulate, or shape, her or his own learning. The brain cannot effectively self-regulate unless it knows what the goals of learning are, where the learner stands on the goals, and how close he or she is to them. (pp. 220, 209)

Once the student receives the feedback, the learning is not over. The learner must apply the feedback in order for it to embed into memory and later transfer to other similar situations. Teachers often bemoan that they have to teach the same concepts students should have learned in previous grades, or even earlier in the same year, but oftentimes, students didn't retain these concepts because either they didn't receive adequate guiding feedback or they didn't apply it to remember it. It is truly a missed opportunity when a teacher provides adequate, accurate, thoughtful feedback but no time for the students to apply it. Scalise and Felde (2017) assert that when students don't have opportunities to learn from and apply feedback, "it is really a failing of the instructional design" (p. 223).

Feedback supports memory formation (Bransford et al. 2000; Jensen, 2005; Medina, 2014; Scalise & Felde, 2017; Sousa, 2016; Whitman & Kelleher, 2016). Jenson (2005) explained that "neural connections are made more efficient by feedback-driven learning. They are made stronger by usage. Combine the two (feedback and usage) and you get a smarter learner" (p. 53). Whitman and Kelleher (2016) asserted that "providing students more frequent, nonthreatening, or low-stakes feedback on their understanding is critical to memory consolidation" (p. 21). To support memory consolidation (transfer to long-term memory), the brain needs to receive feedback, retrieve the original information, integrate the new information, and apply it to a task (e.g., revision). This strengthens neural networks and forms long-term memories which will later transfer to new situations. Feedback also has a critical role in *what* learning gets reinforced. It is often said that "practice makes perfect," but Sousa (2016) and Sprenger (2010) have said that "practice makes *permanent*." Right or wrong, whatever gets practiced gets embedded into memory, which is why it is important that students have opportunities to receive and apply feedback. Feedback increases the likelihood that practice will be accurate. Feedback is therefore "a key component contributing to how our brains develop, and what learning gets reinforced" (Scalise, 2017, p. 33). Using writing as a way to engage students in feedback may include peer feedback through small groups or via digital tools, self-generated feedback through review with a rubric or specific guidelines, blogging, reflective writing, or a test correction paper (described in the next section on writing strategies).

BRAIN-BASED WRITING STRATEGIES TO SUPPORT CONTENT AREA LEARNING

Quick Writes

Quick writes are short, targeted but informal writing tasks or breaks during a lesson to support the learning of content or to informally assess content learning. Having students stop and write about what they are learning keeps the brain focused and strengthens neural pathways by prompting the brain to retrieve, chunk, and convey ideas. A quick write is a "memory enhancer" (Scadden, 2016). Willis (n.d.) affirmed that

> written responses to math or science questions and written predictions, hypotheses, and questions provide all students with the opportunity to actively participate in learning, receive timely feedback, reflect, revise, and risk making mistakes as they build confidence, reveal gaps in foundational knowledge, share creative insights, and build their capacities to communicate their ideas and defend their opinions.

Quick writes can take the form of admit or exit slips, a short list of facts or steps, a brief graphic organizer, a one-paragraph summary, or short answers to 1–3 questions.

Freewriting

Freewriting is a 5–10 minute brainstorming or prewriting strategy that requires the student to write down any and all ideas that come to mind regarding a particular topic. Students may write what they already know, ask questions, or acknowledge a lack of understanding; freewriting is similar to a KWL, but it is more fluid (i.e., stream of consciousness). It requires the student to "attend" to the topic and supports the flow of ideas as the brain retrieves information, makes connections, and creates meaning. There are no "wrong" ideas, so stress is reduced, increasing the likelihood of the amygdala passing information to the prefrontal cortex. This is a priming strategy that activates neural networks and prepares the brain to organize, integrate, prioritize, and synthesize ideas.

Exit Slips

Exit slips are brief end-of-class writing tasks that require students to repeat, reflect, and/or rehearse the day's content. Retrieving, processing, summarizing, or analyzing new content widens neural pathways which support long-term memory of the content (Sousa, 2017). If asked to connect what they've learned to their own lives, the content becomes more relevant, which the brain craves, connecting neural networks to other parts of the brain and increasing the likelihood the content will be remembered. Exit slips can also serve as assessments to help the teacher determine if students grasped the material.

Reader-Response Journal

Reader-response journals engage students in active reading and processing of content by requiring them to state their thoughts, ideas, and or opinions about what they are reading. This taps into the need for the brain to find meaning and relevance in new information. It can capitalize on how emotions enhance memory while activating older memory pathways.

Double-Entry Journals

Double-entry journals are a type of reader-response writing in which students write down content, quotes, or events from a reading on one side of the page, and then on the other, they write their reaction, reflection, or questions. This improves comprehension by requiring students to interact with text, process it, connect their own ideas about it, or form opinions on it. It creates relevance and requires personal connection to the text, two things the brain craves in the meaning-making process. It enhances memory by activating and integrating multiple new and older memory pathways.

Summarizing and Paraphrasing

Summarizing and paraphrasing promote memory-making by requiring the brain to review, rehearse, and repeat, all of which lead to strengthening neural networks leading to long-term memory. These tasks require students to consolidate information and make value judgments about what are the main points. They support understanding and memory as students must create meaning with their own language. "Summarizing is a valuable memory booster" (Willis, 2011a, p. 86).

Test Correction Paper

If students in math class don't reach a designated level of mastery on a test (e.g., 85%), they have the option of completing a test correction paper. Students must find an example in their text that is similar to the item they got wrong and communicate in written words what they should have done to solve the problem, thereby "creating a secondary, language-centered neuron network communicating with the math concept" (Willis, 2011a, p. 94). Once they complete this activity, they earn the opportunity to retake the test. The retake is another opportunity to retrieve and repeat, further strengthening neural pathways memory, and transfer to future math problems.

Peer Feedback

Peer feedback, whether written or via small group dialogue, provides students opportunities to reflect on their own work as they answer questions, consider suggestions, and demonstrate accountability for what they have written. "Greater activation throughout the brain occurs when information is acquired through the diversity of experiences provided by peer collaboration" (Willis, 2011b, para. 15). "When students talk to each other, they get direct feedback on their ideas as well as their behaviors" (Jensen, 2008, p. 195). These shared responses about content benefit both the writer and the reviewer as both must interact with the content. Both must access and retrieve information, discuss it, and clarify or make meaning out of it.

Rubrics

Rubrics "are powerful tools for predictability and patterning" (Willis, 2011a, p. 76). They reduce stress by spelling out the specific criteria used for assessing a learning task. "When learners are provided with a roadmap or framework for the new learning—an overall picture of where they are and where they are going—understanding is enhanced" (Jensen, 2008, p. 196). The brain innately searches for patterns and big pictures. Rubrics take the guesswork out of what the student needs to do to succeed.

Narrative/Storytelling

In order for information to get stored, it has to make sense and it has to have meaning; storytelling is a powerful way to establish both (Jensen, 2005, 2008; Medina, 2014; Scadden, 2016; Scalise & Felde, 2017; Sprenger, 2010). "A picture may be worth a thousand words, but a story is worth all the millennia of attention the human race has devoted to it as an art form—a major mode of transmission for knowledge, principles, and culture" (Scalise, 2017, p. 266). When telling or creating a story, not only are the language centers of the brain activated but any other area of the brain connected to the story will be activated as well (i.e., visual, auditory, emotion, touch). The more areas activated, the more complex the neural networks, and the more opportunities for the brain to retrieve and transfer information. "When all of our senses are stimulated and our emotions aroused, multiple memory pathways are engaged" (Jensen, 2008, p. 163). Perhaps most importantly for content area teachers, when using narrative, whether the teacher is telling the story or students are creating it, learners have opportunities to fully engage the brain while focusing "substantively on curriculum-aligned topics drawing on quantitative thinking, scientific or social studies reasoning, or creative expression" (Scalise, 2017, p. 266).

Blogging

Blogging promotes reflection, critical thinking, choice, relevance, and motivation because of having a real and relevant audience. The social and interactive nature of blogs supports the brain's desire for connections and community. When blogging, students need to provide content to support their views, so they must own their own understandings of the content in order to write about it. They must retrieve previously stored information, make connections, and convey meaning to readers. Others may interact and ask for clarification or pose alternative viewpoints. Numerous free blogging sites for educators offer safe, secure, password-protected environments for students to share their learnings, with no advertising and no student personal information required. Some of these sites include Edublog, Kidblog, and WordPress.

Graphic Organizers, Mind Maps, and Timelines

> Learning is the extraction of meaningful patterns from confusion—in other words, figuring things out in your own way. . . . We never really cognitively understand something until we can create a model or metaphor that is derived from our unique personal world. (Jensen, 2008, p. 168)

Of all the ways the brain receives information, visual processing is the most powerful; 80–90 percent of all information is absorbed by our brains visually. "Visual processing doesn't just assist in the perception of our world. It dominates the perception of our world" (Medina, 2008, p. 224). Graphic organizers, mind maps, and timelines capitalize on the supremacy and potency of visual processing. When thinking graphically, students must retrieve previously stored information, recognize or form patterns, cluster information, ascertain meaningful connections, and visualize relationships. Graphic organizers prompt students to "expand upon existing memory circuitry . . . to create meaningful and relevant connections to previously stored memories" (Willis, 2011a, p. 16) and enable students to "make associations, discover patterns, sort information, and store the new data as relational memories and then long-term memories" (Willis, 2011a, p. 16).

WRITING TO INCORPORATE RELEVANCE

Newspaper editorials, data analysis with discussion, blogging, and argumentative papers engender relevance by providing students opportunities to engage with the content in ways that connect to real-world issues and problems. This connection between personal relevance and the content generates "increased information flow through the attention and emotional filters to the higher processing prefrontal cortex. . . . Even when the facts of the math or science are not debatable, individual responses to the information are appropriate writing topics" (Willis, 2011c, para. 10–11).

REFLECTIVE WRITING

Reflective writing is a memory enhancer (Jensen, 2005, 2008; Scaddan, 2016; Scalise & Felde, 2017; Souse, 2017; Sprenger, 2005; Whitman & Kelleher, 2016). When students are required to think about what they've learned, how they've learned it, and/or how it applies to their own lives, the brain engages in retrieving information, activating older memory pathways, connecting personal relevance, and incorporating feelings regarding content. "In other words, memories with personal meaning are most likely to become relational and long-term memories available for later retrieval" (Willis, 2011a, p. 20). Sprenger (2005) asserted that because it is so effective in supporting memory and content mastery, "reflection is not a luxury; it is a necessity" (p. 38).

CONCLUSION

Given what you now know about how the brain learns and how writing can enhance understanding and memory by engaging the brain in its "highest cognition" (Willis, 2011c), let's revisit your quick write from the beginning of this chapter. What were your three reasons for remembering and choosing the piece of writing that you selected? Could it be said that your piece of writing was relevant to you at the time you wrote it? Did you feel emotionally connected to the writing or the subject? Did you draw from a variety of memories, experiences, senses, or feelings when you wrote it? Did you reflect on it or revise it after it was drafted? Did you receive any feedback, and did that feedback enhance your memory of it or prompt you to improve it? All these months or years later, you still remember this piece and you feel, in some way, connected to it. If this piece of writing mattered to you, and you have a clear memory of its contents, how can you replicate some of those same variables as you consider writing as a tool for learning in your classroom?

Gammill (2006) asserted, "No other exercise in the classroom generates higher thinking skills than does writing" (p. 760). We know that writing is a powerful tool that can be used in the content areas to support myriad of learning activities, including retrieval of prior knowledge, conceptual thinking, critical analysis, recognition of relationships, making personal connections, reflection, tapping emotions, encoding memory, and transferring information to address new problems and challenges. Clearly, writing is thinking. Content area writing is content area thinking. Because of relatively recent research on how the brain learns, we know that neuroplasticity is the principle that the brain is constantly changing, and every time we learn something new, we change the brain (Brown et al., 2014; Jensen, 2005, 2008; Scalise & Felde, 2017; Sousa, 2016, 2017). Teachers who know about neuroplasticity can make intentional instructional decisions with the brain in mind. As John Hattie (2012) reported after examining over 900 studies investigating effective teaching strategies, "Expert teachers . . . believe that intelligence is changeable rather than fixed" (p. 30), and now we know that writing is a brain changer.

REFERENCES

Ambrose, S. A., Bridges, M. W., Lovett, M. C., DiPietro, M., & Norman, M. K. (2010). *How learning works: Seven research-based principles for smart teaching.* Jossey-Bass.

Applebee, A. (1981). Writing in the secondary school: English and the content areas. *NCTE Research Report No. 21.* National Council of Teachers of English.

Bjork, R. A. (1994). Institutional impediments to effective training. In D. Druckman, R. A. Bjork & National Research Council (U.S.). Committee on Techniques for the Enhancement of Human Performance (Eds.), *Learning, remembering, believing: Enhancing human performance.* National Academy Press.

Bransford, J. D., Brown, A. L., & Cocking, R. R. (Eds.). (2000). *How people learn: Brain, mind, experience, and school.* National Academy of sciences.

Brown, P. C., Roediger, H. R., & McDaniel, M. A. (2014). *Make it stick: The science of successful learning.* Harvard University Press.

Clark, R. C., & Mayer, R. E. (2016). *E-learning and the science of instruction.* John Wiley & Sons.

Emig, J. (1977). Writing as a mode of learning. *College Composition and Communication, NCTE, 28*(2), 122–128.

Gammill, D. (2006). Learning the write way. *The Reading Teacher, 59*(8), 754–762.

Hattie, J. (2012). *Visible learning for teachers: Maximizing impact on learning.* Routledge.

Jensen, E. (2008). *Brain-based learning: The new paradigm of teaching* (2nd ed.). Corwin Press.

Jensen, E. (2005). *Teaching with the brain in mind* (2nd ed.). Association for Supervision and Curriculum Development.

Knipper, K. J. & Duggan, T. J. (2006). Writing-to-learn across the curriculum: Tools for comprehension in content area classes. *The Reading Teacher, 59*(5), 462–470.

Medina, J. (2014). *Brain rules: 12 principles for surviving and thriving at work, home, and school.* Pear Press.

Scaddan, M. A. (2016). *40 Engaging brain-based tools for the classroom.* Skyhorse Publishing.

Scalise, K., & Felde, M. (2017). *Why neuroscience matters in the classroom: Principles of brain-based instructional design for teachers.* Pearson.

Sousa, D. A. (2017). *How the brain learns.* Corwin, a Sage Publishing Company.

Sousa, D. A. (2016). *Engaging the rewired brain.* Learning Sciences International.

Sprenger, M. (2010). *Brain-based teaching in the digital age.* Association for Supervision and Curriculum Development.

Sprenger, M. (2005). How to teach so students remember. Association for Supervision and Curriculum Development.

Sullivan, J. (2019, Aug. 13) *On writing and the neuroscience of language.* Brain World. https://brainworldmagazine.com/writing-neuroscience-language/.

Sweller, J. (1988). Cognitive load during problem solving: Effects on learning. *Cognitive Science, 12*, 257–285.

Vygotsky, L. S., & Kozulin, A. (1986). *Thought and language*. Translation newly rev. and edited by Alex Kozulin. MIT Press.

Whitman, G. & Kelleher, I. (2016). *Neuro teach: Brain science and the future of education.* Rowan & Littlefield.

Willis, J. (n.d.) *Why all students should write: A neurological explanation.* Teach thought. https://www.teachthought.com/literacy/why-all-students-should-write-a-neurological-explanation-for-literacy/.

Willis, J. (2011a). *Researched-based strategies to ignite student learning*. Association for Supervision and Curriculum Development.

Willis, J. (2011b, May 3). *Writing and the brain: Neuroscience shows the pathways to learning.* National Writing Project. https://archive.nwp.org/cs/public/print/resource/3555?x-print_friendly=1&x-print_friendly=1.

Willis, J. (2011c, July 11). *The Brain-based benefits of writing for math and science learning.* Edutopia. https://www.edutopia.org/blog/writing-executive-function-brain-research-judy-willis.

Willis, J. A. (2017, Sept. 12). *The neuroscience of narratives for memory. Edutopia.* https://www.edutopia.org/article/neuroscience-narrative-and-memory.

Chapter 3

Writing as a Tool for Social Change

Ebony Perez and Christina Cazanave

THE SIGNIFICANCE OF BIAS-FREE LANGUAGE IN WRITING

In today's classrooms students need the knowledge and skills to be able to share experiences and feelings, and insights about a variety of topics. Educators can support and encourage students to respectfully discuss issues and ideas about historical and contemporary issues. Teaching students to be aware of both individual and systemic injustices, bias, and of the impact past injustice has on our current experiences engages their critical thinking as well as creative skills. Intentional focus on social justice topics exposes students to the array of potential pathways to combat injustice, including advocacy and activism, thus inspiring students to become agents of positive change. As students learn to engage in antibias thinking guided curricula activities can allow students the opportunity to uncover their potential to effect change. One critical step toward being an effective change agent is discovering how to improve our bias-free language skills.

Cultural influences can shape our writing in many ways. When speaking, our facial expressions and gestures may signal we are not being offensive. However, in writing, it is a lot harder to do. Teaching students how to examine their own ideas and civilly respond to the views of their peers who may not share their opinions is an important lifelong skill. Educators can provide students with the opportunity to learn to work together toward a common goal. Before you read this chapter, read the following statements and decide if you agree or disagree with each statement. At the end of the chapter, we will revisit these statements.

1. The rules for appropriate, standard written expression are well established and have remained constant for many years.
2. Critical thinking is necessary for successful bias-free writing.
3. Self-reflection enables you to improve bias recognition.
4. Language is a powerful and evolving tool.
5. Writing might reflect prejudicial beliefs or perpetuate assumptions even if we do not recognize them.
6. Bias-free language in writing is equally as important as clarity, grammar, spelling, and accuracy.

Writing is a powerful tool that shapes our world by guiding our thoughts, sharing our feelings, stimulating creativity, expressing ideas, and inspiring change. No matter the topic or genre, writing can transfigure you into a change agent. Writing is one way we reveal stories and impart knowledge about ourselves and others. It is a tool for transformation, which can help us name our truth, face fears, and empower our decision-making. As a teacher, no matter what subject you teach, you have the opportunity to show your students how they may fulfill their mission and purpose through pen and paper or behind the keyboard. Teachers can find and develop writing exercises that foster an awareness of difference, power, and discrimination. This chapter provides exercises and tips for helping your students developing bias-free writing.

JEFF'S WRITING SAMPLE

Jeff, a seventh-grade student at Holman Middle School, is a reporter for his school newspaper. He attended a press conference about a local fire and submitted the following article for the school paper to Ms. Canton, his teacher.

City Hall was packed as the crowd pushed into the auditorium to hear the firemen report about the destruction caused by yesterday's fire. In the ruckus, as the mob rushed into the auditorium, a wheelchair-bound disabled person was knocked over.

Because of the extent of the devastating event, the stage was crowded with firemen and councilmen. The press conference began with a Negro fireman explaining that during the blaze fifty elderly residents' homes had been destroyed when the low-income housing was demolished. Eager to capture exact quotes, each of the reporters eagerly grabbed his/her notepad and began writing.

The entire building, including the fifty residences within the building, would need to be totally demolished. A right-winged fanatic asked if the building had been limited to elderly occupants. The final speaker must have had a blonde moment because, at the end of the meeting as everyone was being dismissed, she remembered to finally provide the address of the residence that had been destroyed.

What concerns, if any, do you have about Jeff's article? Should Ms. Canton run the story in the paper as is? After reading the chapter decide how you would suggest Jeff rewrite his article.

INTRODUCTION TO BIAS-FREE LANGUAGE

As a writer, we strive to create expressive writing that provides information, persuades, or creates a literary work (New Palts, 2014). In all cases, we must approach our work with integrity and accuracy, ensuring we do not isolate our readers with language that propagates prejudicial beliefs or stereotypical attitudes. Instead, we strive to use bias-free language that shows respect, is factual, and incorporates inclusivity when discussing ability, age, gender, gender identification, immigration status, racial and ethnic identity, sexual orientation, socioeconomic status, and other personal factors (University of Wisconsin Madison, n.d.). When utilizing bias-free language, we are still incorporating appropriate spelling, grammar, and syntactic structure. Yet, tools such as critical thinking, self-reflection, and language development are equally crucial to the writing process, especially when discussing topics that tend to be stereotyped or generalized. Bias-free language is clear, nonjudgmental, and stereotype free (Northern Illinois University, n.d.). Learning to utilize these tools can assist educators in raising consciousness of their students and show what antibias attitudes and behaviors look like in the classroom.

CRITICAL THINKING

Critical thinking involves asking questions regarding the meaning behind a statement, claim, or argument. Perhaps the simplest definition is offered by Ennis (2011), who defines this style of thinking as "reasonable, reflective thinking that is focused on deciding what to believe or do" (p. 5). These important skills are used to assess evidence and evaluate arguments in mass media, social media, academic papers, research findings, or conversational debates. In essence, critical thinking allows us to step back, look at the situation from different viewpoints, and discard quick judgment or decisions until all information is collected.

To think critically, we must learn to face the discomfort of the unknown. For example, critical thinkers need to think skeptical, remain open minded, search for evidence, appreciate clarity, and be willing to change opinions when evidence supports a different position (Moore, 2013). Thinking critically does not mean questioning everything, but instead, it focuses on assessing statements based on a set of criteria. For example, does the statement include accurate facts, site credible sources, and use unbiased language? If not, it is essential to evaluate, examine, and deconstruct the argument to determine if it is a blanketed statement that is vague asserting a premise without providing evidence or is it a statement supported by factual evidence.

Critical thinking is a tool to help us grow and adapt. It is not just for the purpose of finding flaws, justifying a point, or creating division. Instead, it enables a person to feel much more confident in their conclusions. To effectively begin this higher-order thinking, we must accept that not everything we see and hear is factual and based on evidence. In accepting this thought, we must utilize and analyze the information to form a judgment.

Reflective thinking is important and requires us to ask questions about the material presented. For example, we should ask questions such as "how does the author know this information," or "is there another side to the argument," or "what information is missing." Furthermore, questioning the sources by asking where the information comes from and how it was gathered is key to the process. Lastly, critical thinking encompasses not being afraid to point out biased language or other actions. Yet, to ask these tough questions and begin this evaluation, we must mitigate our unconscious or confirmation bias to best ensure that our ability for evidence-based reflection is not clouded.

THE IMPORTANCE OF SELF-REFLECTION

As we grow in critical thinking and evaluation, we cannot overlook that everyone has an unconscious or conscious bias that may impact our assessment of information (Navarro, n.d.). These thoughts can obscure our ability to report or identify all the facts. In other words, data is consciously or unconsciously left out and specific points are not presented. A bias is defined as a prejudice for or against one thing, a person, or group over another (Merriam-Webster, 2021). It can be an inaccurate and unfair judgment. Unconscious bias means we are not fully aware of our bias, but these thoughts still impact our words and actions. Unfortunately, biases can lead to inaccurate assumptions, such as damaging stereotypes or the dismissal of divergent viewpoints. For example, a person may uphold a stereotype that individuals on government assistant programs are lazy. After hearing this statement, you may agree because of a bad experience you had with a person who was on government assistance and could not maintain a long-term job. Despite evidence-based studies stating the opposite, you may continue to uphold this belief based on this one experience.

We must also be aware of seeking out information that will uphold, reiterate, or justify our argument (New Literacy Project, n.d.), also known as confirmation bias. Confirmation bias diminishes new information as false or inaccurate simply because it does not support your point of view. Examples of confirmation bias can be seen throughout social media. Do you know a person who only posts about their ideological side? Do they actively defend their side no matter what the subject or evidence presented? This person is acting on their confirmation bias. When confirmation bias influences how we find and share information, we risk getting an incomplete and inaccurate picture of an issue, event, or topic.

To be an influential writer, we must use self-reflection to determine how we come to know information, feel about a topic, and reflect on purposely avoiding an opposing viewpoint. When ruminating on these areas, we are countering any form of bias by recognizing it in ourselves. When we are open to admitting the bias we hold, we can guard against it by using a wide range of credible sources, reading opinions from various positions, and including multiple perspectives in our writing. The usage of self-reflection means we can improve our writing and weigh in on situations with more confidence and accuracy.

LANGUAGE EVOLUTION

Language is dynamic and shifts as our society evolves. Language is not only a way for us to express concepts and ideas, but it is also a way for us to affect thoughts (Zegada, 2020). Understanding the power of words is key to both critical thinking and self-reflection. We have inherited a system that routinely—and often unconsciously—reinforces prejudicial beliefs. We all know and have used terms and phrases that perpetuate negativity and stereotypes, such as when someone is told they "run like a girl" or are "acting gay." Prevailing societal attitudes influence all of us; therefore, we all have the responsibility to unlearn the misinformation we have absorbed about others.

We can all benefit from examining the language we use around diversity and learn to use empowering language. Historically, when discussing diversity, we primarily focused on gender and race. We have grown as a society and recognize that all of us hold multiple identities. These identities are often simultaneously dominant as well as marginalized. As we look at how our expanded various identities, including age, ethnicity, religion, sexual orientation, immigrant status, and more, shape our lives, we can begin to break the divisions among us. Doing so requires word and language tools. We need to know how to name the things around us and understand the deeply rooted dynamics of dominance in ageism, classism, racism, sexism, and heterosexism that create anger, hurt, and other powerful emotions.

The words we use affect and reveal how we think about and value others. Language can be both a tool of oppression and freedom. We have all learned about the various "isms" in our world. Awareness of the phrases that convey otherness, criticism, judgments, such as "you or those people" increases the opportunity for us to shift our understanding of people. All of our lives, we have learned to do difficult tasks through failures and successes. We have learned to read, ride a bike, drive a car, and more without allowing our mistakes to get in the way of trying again. Allowing ourselves and others the grace and space to unlearn the ways we have been misinformed about one another allows us to create a more just society.

GUIDING PRINCIPLES FOR WRITING BIAS-FREE

As we discussed, language is not neutral. Using words that convey understanding is not to be done because we want to be "correct" but because we recognize how we use language affects how we see ourselves and others. It begins with using terminology that individuals use to describe themselves. We can incorporate these terminologies by simply asking people how they prefer to be referenced or avoiding nouns or assumptions when information is unknown. For example, avoid using terminology such as homosexual when discussing sexual identity. Instead, utilize language such as gay, lesbian, gender-fluid, as this language specifies the identity instead of generalizing that all individuals feel and identify the same way (American Psychological Association, 2019).

Another principle to consider is grammar, like language, evolves. One of the most widely discussed grammatical changes is the singular use of "they." In some instances, it may be intuitive to use "they" in a sentence. For example, you should not use masculine pronouns when the gender of a person is unknown. Instead, use "they" when you are unsure or unaware of a person's gender or it is irrelevant to the context (American Psychological Association, 2019). As in "Please, ask someone if they can help get the bike from the top shelf." However, writers should also use the singular "they" when the person uses "they" as their pronoun (American Psychological Association, 2019; Merriam-Webster Dictionary, 2019). For instance, "Charlie has a mid-term, but they haven't begun to study." This reflects and honors how Charlie sees themselves as nonbinary and communicates that in our language and writing.

While these grammar and language changes may feel awkward at first, evolution is clumsy. So keep trying. We need to know how to describe the world around us, and any blame or guilt from not getting it just right is unfair to you and those you are teaching. We can learn to use language to empower and inform those around us. When writing, we must create reminders to check our usage of language that incorporates the practices below.

FOCUS ON RELEVANT CHARACTERISTICS

Precision in our writing is a critical piece of bias-free writing. When referring to people, we need to use accurate, clear, and free of prejudicial implications. Although it is easy to describe a person by age, gender, race, or other characteristics, it is not always necessary. Determine which characteristics are important and appropriate to highlight in your writing. Think of the details that are needed to improve the reader's understanding of your work. If you are writing a creative piece, details about age, gender, and race are vital details that need to be incorporated into the story. However, if you are creating a science scenario, "the researcher" collecting data may not need to describe them with details such as gender, age, and race. The proper choice of which specific details to include depends on the situation. When including such details, remember that particular characteristics should be provided to give clarity to your audience.

Another essential factor in writing without bias is acknowledging relevant differences when they do exist. Those differences should highlight the target of the situation and not how the group differs from the dominant group. An example of this would be evaluating the range of math test scores in a group of students. Is it relevant to the situation to examine the difference in scores between the girls and boys? If so, then describe the difference.

HUMANITY OVER LABELS—PUTTING THE PERSON FIRST

We may inadvertently label individuals when we use adjectives as collective nouns to describe groups. Phrases such as "the autistic students," "the mentally ill," or "the poor" should be avoided as they do not convey respect or sensitivity to their individual lived experiences. Instead, it would be best to use descriptive language (i.e., people with learning differences, people living in poverty). Using person-first language focuses on the person rather than the circumstances impacting their lives. It also helps avoid falling into the trap of using negative or condescending metaphors that can be regarded as slurs (i.e., nuts, cripple) or excessively negative (brain-damaged, special needs) as well as ineffective in the description of an individual (i.e., high functioning).

Expect and accept that language changes over time, and how people refer to themselves and others will continue to evolve as well. This continuous change is not a new phenomenon. One illustration of this is the labels that people of African descent have been referred to in the United States. The terms colored, Negro, Black, Afro-American, and African American have all been used. The shifting of these terms reflects the historical time point in which they were widely utilized. Calling someone "colored" in this historical time point would likely be highly offensive. Another example is the language we use around people with learning differences. It was common to refer to people as mentally retarded, slow, simpleminded, or deaf and dumb at one point in time. These terms are currently viewed as outdated and stigmatizing as we have come to focus on the learner and not on their diagnosis.

TOOLS FOR BIAS-FREE WRITING

The evolution in how we use language can be further illustrated when considering how the terms we use related to gender identity and sexual orientation have changed. Knowing when and how to use terms related to gender and sex is key to avoiding bias when discussing this topic. So let's talk about the terms.

Gender is a social construct that refers to the attitudes, behaviors, and feelings that a culture associates with an individual's biological sex (APA, 2012). *Sex*, however, refers to the physical parts—or birth sex—a person is born with. Another key term is *gender identity*, which applies to all of us, and is distinctly different from sexual orientation. It describes one's innate feelings about their own gender. Gender may or may not match the sex assignment one received at birth. When one's gender identity conforms to their assigned sex, this is known as a person being cisgendered. If an individual does not identify as *cisgender*, they may identify as either transgender or nonconforming. *Transgender* is an adjective used to describe a person whose gender identity does not align. Understanding each of these terms will help in deciding what words should be used in describing persons, communities, and populations.

Students need to develop language that affirms their multiple identity groups as well as to accurately and respectfully describe how people (including themselves) are both similar to and different from each other (Teaching Tolerance, 2016). Bias-free writing also incorporates writing that avoids jargon or terms often used as adjectives that uphold stereotypes (Heaps, n.d). For example, a person may use the statement "having a blonde moment" as a reference to making a mistake or causing an accident. These phrases are

Table 3.1 Bias-Free Terms

Terms to Avoid	*Possible Terms to Use*	*Explanation*
Minorities	People of Color, marginalized, underrepresented groups, racial minorities	Minorities is a word that has broader implications than numbers and is often incorrectly and inaccurately applied
Illegal Alien Illegal	Undocumented individual	Using "illegal" or "alien" refers that a human being is illegal or without rights
Black person White person	Black White	Racial and ethnic groups are designated by proper nouns and are capitalized
Mexican woman Black man	the woman the man	Only include the nationality where it is relevant
Hispanic	Latino, Latina, Latin, or Latinx (as gender-neutral or nonbinary)	Use the inclusive gender or specific ethnic if known (Colombian, Puerto Rican, etc.)
Homosexual	Gay, Lesbian, Queer, Bisexual	Homosexual historically has carried pejorative stereotypes
Autistic Epileptic Disabled	Person with autism Person with epilepsy Person with a disability	The person should be referred to before the other characteristic
Ethnic, racial, cultural slurs	Describe the action accurately	Ethnicity, race, or culture does not describe actions
Seniors, the aged, elderly, senile	Older adults, people sixty-five and older, the older population	These terms typically connate negativity, stereotypes

easily understood but still offensive to different individuals, populations, communities, and cultures. Table 3.1 should be used as a guide to help writers select appropriate terms and phrases that best meet antibias language.

These principles should not be taken as an all-inclusive list or checklist; however, they should be considered a beginning to working toward bias-free language in our writing. Just as you are taking time to learn the new things presented here, we will discover additional things as we move toward a more just and harmonious society. Now let us revisit the statements from the beginning of the chapter.

1. The rules for appropriate, standard written expression are well established and have remained constant for many years.
2. Critical thinking is a component of successful bias-free writing.
3. Self-reflection enables you to improve bias recognition.
4. Language is a powerful and evolving tool.
5. Writing might imply prejudicial beliefs or perpetuate assumptions even if we do not recognize them.

6. Bias-free language in writing is equally as important as clarity, grammar, spelling, and accuracy.

In what ways has your thinking changed about these statements? What are you most concerned about when it comes to bias-free writing? What three techniques or strategies will you implement to decrease bias in your writing? How does bias-free writing connect to confronting social injustice?

As you critically reflect and respond to the above statements and questions, you are moving along the path of reducing bias in your work. This will often extend beyond your writing and make its way into your oral communication as well. Soon enough, you will be modeling for others and creating change in subtle yet powerful ways.

SERVICE-LEARNING: WRITING TO ADDRESS A SOCIAL ISSUE

Service-learning is defined as an experiential learning strategy that helps students move knowledge beyond the classroom and apply critical thinking to the real world (Loyola University Chicago, n.d.; Suffolk University, n.d.). One of the strategies is writing. In recognizing their own agency students become aware of their own responsibility to stand up to exclusion, prejudice, and injustice. No matter the content area, writing is a critical skill that students need to bring theory into practice.

Some people are passionate about using their voices to bring attention to social issues such as poverty, climate change, systematic racism, and so on. The purpose of this writing is to persuade and inform others on the needs of the problem. Even though our intention may be honorable, it is essential when using this style of writing that we are not providing confirmation bias material that does not reflect divergent viewpoints or isolates populations or communities. To avoid this, we must intentionally set aside our agenda and be honest in our description of the problem (Bennet, 2015). For example, we may write an opinion piece that details the impact of ignoring climate change. However, to provide a complete picture of the issue, we must address the hesitancy of coal miners and their fear of losing employment, income, and housing stability.

Providing a comprehensive view of the issue does not lose your main message; instead, it offers bipartisan information so readers can begin to create and evaluate solutions (University of Florida, 2015). For example, we may write a letter to our state legislator about the decrease of affordable housing in our community. We must provide clear points that address the housing crisis without using language that blames, threatens, or misleads facts to move our point across. Instead, we must remember the tools of critical thinking, self-reflection, and bias-free terminology to ensure we are influencing others for the greater good. There are many creative ways to bring these types of activities into the classroom. Below are some activities you may want to try or to adapt to fit your content needs.

- Write stories about the history of your school or town for a class project to share with the school.
- Investigate a community need, write a comprehensive report using county or state data, start an awareness campaign.
- Analyze data about local pollution levels and write a report on the impact to your town or state.
- Find, interview, and write the histories of diverse people in your community.
- Conduct water sampling of local waterways (streams, lakes, ponds, etc.) and provide results.

The possibilities for service-learning projects are immense. The examples above are just starting points that can be tailored to fit your class, content area, or age of students. These tools may help practitioners and students jumpstart their own ideas about a project of their own. Combining academic goals with community service deepens the learning opportunities and empowers students to tackle community issues and make positive changes in their families, peers, and community.

JEFF'S ARTICLE REVISITED

After reading this chapter, decide how you would help Jeff reword his article. His original article follows.

City Hall was packed as the crowd pushed into the auditorium to hear the firemen report about the destruction caused by yesterday's fire. In the ruckus, as the mob rushed into the auditorium, a wheelchair-bound disabled person was knocked over.

Because of the extent of the devastating event, the stage was crowded with firemen and councilmen. The press conference began with a Negro fireman explaining that during the blaze fifty elderly residents' homes had been destroyed when the low-income housing was demolished. Eager to capture exact quotes, each of the reporters eagerly grabbed his notepad and began writing.

The entire building, including the fifty residences within the building, would need to be totally demolished. A right-winged fanatic asked if the building had been limited to elderly occupants. The final speaker must have had a blonde moment, because at the end of the meeting as everyone was being dismissed, that she remembered to finally provide the address of the residence that had been destroyed.

CONCLUSION

Language has, is, and will continue to be dynamic. Cultural influences and practices have shaped how we use language in both overt and subtle ways. Critical thinking and self-reflection are vital components to unlearning how we have perpetuated stereotypes, disrespect, and inadvertently sown hurt and mistrust into our communities. The good news is with awareness comes opportunity. We have the opportunity to acknowledge our missteps without guilt or shame and create space for others to do the same. How we write about ourselves and others speaks volumes regarding how we value individuals, groups, and even ourselves. For when you are confident in who you are, you allow others the chance to live in their truth. Bias-free writing is not about being "politically correct." However, it is a way for us to be the author of more authentic stories that make space for more diversity, inclusivity, and justice.

REFERENCES

Benner, L. (2015). 3 Insights into writing about social issues. https://www.janefriedman.com/writing-about-social-issues/.

de Onís, C. M. (2017). What's in an "x"? An exchange about the politics of "Latinx." Chiricú *Journal: Latina/o Literatures, Arts, and Cultures, 1*(2), 78–91. https://doi.org/10.2979/chiricu.1.2.07.

Ennis, R. (2011). Critical thinking: Reflection and perspective, part 2. *Inquiry: Critical Thinking across the Disciplines, 26*(2), 5–19.

Heaps, S. (n.d.). Bias examples. https://www.writeexpress.com/bias.html.

Loyola University Chicago. (n.d.). Ignatian pedagogy and service-learning. https://www.luc.edu/experiential/service-learning/service-learningpedagogy/.

Merriam-Webster. (n.d.). Bias. In Merriam-Webster.com dictionary. https://www.merriam-webster.com/dictionary/bias.

Merriam-Webster. (2019). Words we're watching: Singular "they" though singular "they" is old, "they" as a nonbinary pronoun is new—and useful. https://www.merriam-webster.com/words-at-play/singular-nonbinary-they.

Moore, T. (2013). Critical thinking: Seven definitions in search of a concept. *Studies in Higher Education, 38*(4), 506–522.

Navarro, J. R. (n.d.). What is unconscious bias. UCSF Office of Diversity and Outreach. https://diversity.ucsf.edu/resources/unconscious-bias.

News Literacy Project. (n.d.). Did you know? Don't let confirmation bias narrow your perspective. https://newslit.org/tips-tools/dont-let-confirmation-bias-narrow-your-perspective/.
New Paltz. (2014). Module: The writing process understanding the four major purposes for writing. https://sites.newpaltz.edu/owrc/wp-content/uploads/sites/16/2014/01/Purpose-Handout.pdf.
Northern Illinois University. (n.d.). Effective writing practices tutorial. https://www.niu.edu/writingtutorial/style/bias-free-language.shtml.
Reflective Thinking. (n.d.). Reflective thinking: RT. https://www.hawaii.edu/intlrel/pols382/Reflective%20Thinking%20-%20UH/reflection.html#:~:text=Critical%20thinking%20and%20reflective%20thinking%20are%20often%20used%20synonymously.&text=In%20summary%2C%20critical%20thinking%20involves,judgments%20about%20what%20has%20happened.
Suffolk University. (n.d.). What is service-learning? https://www.suffolk.edu/student-life/student-involvement/community-public-service/service-learning/what-is-service-learning.
Teaching Tolerance. (2016). Social Justice Standards: The Teaching Tolerance anti-bias framework. A Project of the Southern Poverty Law Center.
University of Florida. (2015). Teaching students to solve social problems. https://education.ufl.edu/behavior-management-resource-guide/2015/01/16/teaching-students-to-solve-social-problems/.
University of Wisconsin Madison. (n.d.). A guide to bias-free communications. https://academicaffairs.ucsd.edu/_files/aps/adeo/Article_Guide_to_Bias-Free_Communications.pdf.
Zegada, M. (2020). More than words: How language affects the way we think. https://www.gofluent.com/blog/how-language-affects-the-way-we-think/.

Chapter 4

Writing as a Snapshot of Thinking

Holly S. Atkins, Kim Higdon, and Nakita Gillespie

TO BEGIN

Consider your own writing history as a K–12 student. Do you have a box or scrapbook filled with pieces of writing your mom carefully saved? What about the papers that filled your locker and the bottom of your backpack? Think about the writing you did in elementary–middle–high school. If you wrote the story of you as a K–12 student writer, what would you say? Do that now. Craft your writing memoir. In six words. Just six words.

The traditional view of writing entails the composition of texts in formats such as narrative, expository, analytical, persuasive, and argumentative that employ conventions and elements based on classical Greek and Latin teachings. Even in the classical view, the tools used in composition have expanded with technology, but the conventions and formats are generally static. As the world has evolved, thinking about learning does too. The internet ushered in the Information Age, changing learning by giving people more actionable means of acquiring almost limitless amounts of information. With the advancement of artificial intelligence, we are moving into the Innovation Age (Tan et al., 2006). The work of learning moves from a passive idea of filling a container with information to inquiry and knowledge building (Bereiter & Scardamalia, 1996). Indicators of a knowledge-building approach to learning are student agency in building a repertoire of skills and knowledge based on their needs and interests, multidisciplinary learning, performance-based assessments to evaluate understanding and growth, collaborative, and recursive (Tan et al., 2006). Additionally, in the arena of composition, societal changes and rapid expansion of technologies at our disposal have increased the modalities of expression from oral and writing traditions to "visual, audio, gestural, spatial, or linguistic means of creating meaning"

(Selfe, 2007, p. 195). To further muddy the waters, expression can employ multiple modalities in a single composition, an idea that will be explored more fully in this chapter.

PROCESS AND PRODUCT

This brings us to the idea of process and product. A process can be defined as the steps taken to achieve a particular goal or end. Processes are dynamic and fluid, adventures that involve questions and decisions that may potentially lead to detours, dead ends, and almost certainly, more questions. Products are the artifacts of processes, and they are a snapshot in time. They are the way students show what they know. While the classical view of learning would posit that it is the final product is all that matters, it is, in essence, the culmination of the learning and interpretation of knowledge; constructivists, or people who support a knowledge-building view of learning, would argue that it is in the process where knowledge building happens. The process vs. product debate is akin to the old chicken and egg question. The truth is, it does not matter; aren't we glad they are both here? As teachers, we need to see evidence of learning and evaluate our students' learning, and therefore the products are goal posts that help us with that work. As facilitators of learning, processes are critical as well; without process, there is no product. Our view, and the perspective moving forward, is that both process and product are essential in the classroom, and both are addressed in this chapter.

Our goal is not to debate the merits of the classical view or the modern view; to the contrary, we would argue that both have their place in the classroom. However, taking an inclusive view means learning can be messy. Some prefer to avoid a mess. But consider stepping into a rain puddle. This can track dirt and water and make your socks wet and feel annoying and aggravating. At the same time, it can be joyful and invite a sense of wonder as you splash around in delight. As you dig into the messiness of learning, we hope that you will take a playful approach as you consider the ideas in this chapter and all your work in the classroom.

ENGAGING STUDENTS IN COMPLEX, NOT SUPERFICIAL LEARNING

When we value the process as we do the product and become willing to step in the rain puddle, we allow students the opportunity to grapple with their learning in a way that builds deep, long-lasting connections. More importantly, when we pair this student ownership of the writing process with topics and modalities that are authentic to students, we set them up to feed their appetite for learning. In the words of Ken Robinson (2016), "Young children have a ready appetite to explore whatever draws their interest. When their curiosity is engaged, they will learn for themselves, from each other, and from any source they can lay their hands on" (p. 135). Further, when utilizing writing as a performance assessment, we can increase student motivation, allow students to develop their own area of interest, use critical thinking skills, and engage students in hands-on learning—promoting long-term learning (Banks, 2012).

In the traditional school model, learning happens in silos. A science teacher teaches science, a history teacher who teaches history, and an English teacher who teaches reading and writing. Everyone stays neatly in their lane. But real life doesn't come in silos. Language is a part of every discipline—even the most basic learning involves a teacher talking to students. Take, for example, the COVID-19 pandemic of 2020. When teachers make informed decisions about what actions need to be taken requires an understanding of scientific concepts about viruses and vaccinations. Knowledge of the historical and political contexts of government, medicine, and the pharmaceutical industry may play into decision-making. Comprehending information through listening and reading and the interpretation of statistical information would be critical. Perhaps most importantly, evaluating copious amounts of conflicting information, including the credibility of who is presenting the information, and measuring that information against personal values and beliefs, all go into making the decisions that directly and profoundly impact daily life. Real life demands interdisciplinary, complex thinking.

Objective tests are restrictive, limited to what the teacher expects the student should know. A written response is open ended, creative, allowing students to express what they know, have learned, or have yet to learn. When a teacher reads a child's writing, they access an open window and become privy to the inner workings of a student's learning experience. A writing piece not only reveals what a person knows and understands, but also what ideas or information that person values, what they wonder, and more (Graves, 2002). Unlike traditional assessments, these powerful writing opportunities provide a continued, meaningful learning experience for students while also allowing teachers the opportunity to assess student learning outcomes.

Writing as an authentic demonstration of learning can present in a way that may seem unconventional, even in the world of writing. Rather than repeating the traditional writing formats discussed earlier, teachers should invite students to engage in complex thinking by utilizing multimedia, multimodal, and unexpected product formats. When students are encouraged to grapple with their learning over an extended period, like with this process of writing, they are developing their "long thinking" abilities (Graves, 2002). Learning is unique and complex. Open-ended writing projects allow the student to explore their learning and have the autonomy to make the small choices that lead to big outcomes.

STUDENTS AS CREATORS

Fundamental to our perspective on writing as a production or demonstration of learning is the role of the student. Writing as both process and product involves engaged students actively creating, which of course leads to a product. Consider figure 4.1.

Here, the familiar revised Bloom's Taxonomy of Learning (Anderson et al., 2001) pyramid is reformatted. The higher-level thinking skills of creating, analyzing, and evaluating work symbiotically are informed by the lower-level thinking skills. The higher-level thinking skills becoming the focus and catalyst for all other levels of learning. It is important to remember that Benjamin Bloom (Bloom et al., 1956) never intended the pyramid to be viewed as a step-by-step progression of learning, but rather an identification of levels of cognitive processes. When writing is used as

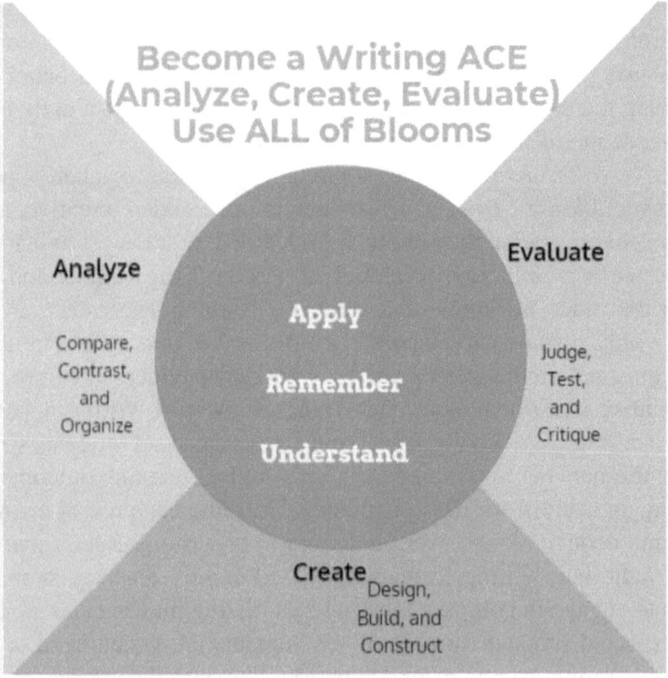

Figure 4.1 Targeted Bloom's Pyramid.

a production and demonstration of learning, the act of writing is an act of creation. Students creating writing to reflect their learning engage in all levels of Bloom's cognitive processes. Crafting their writing, students draw upon (remembering) information presented in lectures, texts, discussions. They apply this to their writing when they understand the information. What information is included, why, and how involves the writer in analyzing and evaluating. Is this a different process from studying for a test? Absolutely. Assessment becomes an opportunity to deepen learning, to get it all into long-term memory.

SMALL WRITING, BIG THINKING

When they hear the word writing, people tend to think of writing papers—long, wordy research papers, position papers, or even more creative, but also challenging, creative endeavors like fiction or poetry writing. Teachers, especially those who teach content other than English/Language Arts, wonder how they will have time in an already-packed curriculum. Students are hesitant because they feel they lack the skills or interest in this kind of writing. The good news for teachers and students is that writing does not have to be long and arduous to impact, enhance, or demonstrate learning. In this section, we explain how using micro writing or quick writes can profoundly affect students' thinking and learning.

Let's begin by defining micro writing, also known as quick writing. Micro writing is a short classroom activity that takes anywhere from 1 to 10 minutes of writing time (Ferlazzo, 2018; Rief, 2018). The writing is informal and is done without censoring, focusing on ideas rather than formats or conventions (Rief, 2018). It may, but does not have to, involve prompts and scaffolds. When followed by discussion, quick writes can be a way to help students process and articulate their learning, understandings, assumptions, and questions about any given topic (Brookfield, 2012). Teachers can use micro writings to check for understanding, evaluate the depth of understanding of a topic, clarify misunderstandings, and inform practices for future learning (Brookfield, 2012; Christopher, 2018; Ferlazzo, 2018). Without putting debilitating stress on students or diverting time away from other classroom activities, used skillfully, micro writing can have a profound and valuable impact on learning. While quick writes/micro writings are short, informal, and low stress, they can generate higher-level thinking. In quick writing, especially when paired with discussion, students create, evaluate, analyze, and apply ideas, knowledge, and thinking.

In addition to fostering critical thinking (Brookfield, 2012; Christopher, 2018; Felazzo, 2018; Rief, 2018), the benefits of micro writing include:

- Activation of background knowledge (Ferlazzo, 2018)

  Helping students clarify thinking and finding their voice (Christopher, 2018; Ferlazzo, 2018; Ritchhart et al., 2011; Rief, 2018)

  Enabling students to reflect on and transfer learning (Brookfield, 2012; Ferlazzo, 2018; Ritchhart et al., 2011)
- Expand student metacognition and examination of assumptions (Brookfield, 2012; Christopher, 2018; Ritchhart et al., 2011)
- Encouraging creative and visual thinking (Felazzo, 2018; Ritchhart et al., 2011)
- Fostering a culture of collaborative learning (Brookfield, 2012; Christopher, 2018; Felazzo, 2018; Ritchhart et al., 2011)
- Causes less stress for English learners (Felazzo, 2018) and students who are not confident writers

In a nutshell, micro writing is like Hermia in A Midsummer's Night Dream: "Though she be but little, she is fierce." Following are some ideas for using micro writing in the classroom.

THE SIX-WORD MEMOIR

Students love six-word memoirs because, well, they are only six words. By limiting it to six words, students have to pare down their writing to one big idea and carefully choose words that will best express their message. It's a win-win situation; students think they are doing a little work, but teachers know they are doing deep thinking. This exercise began as memoirs, which can still be an effective way to connect with your students and their lives (Christopher, 2018). Teens can even read and publish their six-word memoirs on the site sixwordmemoirs.com. (Note: The language is not censored.)

Six-word memoirs have evolved past an actual memoir, though. Teachers can assign a six-word "memoir" in response to a question or prompt. Students can write from the perspective of a character, historical figure, or someone with a different viewpoint than themselves. Teachers can ask students to explain a math procedure, scientific concept, or historical event (Rich, 2014). As with the minute paper, this is a practice that can be adapted to a variety of contexts for a variety of purposes.

Examples: Some animals are much more equal.

Slavery abolished but enter Jim Crow
Airplanes side by side, parallel (hopefully)
Virus on monkey kidneys, byeee polio!
Just trying to get by lately

BOIL IT DOWN

Teachers know, and standardized test scores verify that summarizing or being able to pick out the essential points from information is a challenging skill for students. Yet, it is critical in both receptive and expressive communication. Being able to quickly discern the big ideas from the details is necessary for effective note-taking and essential in activities that require higher-level thinking, such as analysis, synthesis, and evaluation. This can be an effective strategy to help students record their thinking and then repeatedly analyze the content to boil it down to the most important idea. This can be done with or without a prompt or question. First, students record their thoughts on an index card. Then, using a second smaller piece of paper (a sticky note or an index card that has been cut to a smaller size), students boil those thoughts down to fit on the smaller paper (without changing the size of their writing). Then they repeat on a smaller note. Students can then discuss their most important ideas with a small group or with the class. For detailed directions, see the link shared in the "Further Explorations" section of this chapter.

3–2–1 REFLECTION

The 3–2–1 reflection is a strategy used to write down six thoughts about learning. This is frequently presented in a graphic organizer, and the teacher asks three questions. Three common questions that can be applied universally are as follows:

1. What are three things I learned about _______?
2. What are two questions I have about ______?
3. What is the most important thing I learned?

This set of prompts, done at the end of a learning cycle, is more metacognitive (Christopher, 2018):

1. Three things I learned
2. Two things I already knew
3. One way I changed my thinking

Figure 4.2 provides an example of a possible format for arranging a 3–2–1 graphic organizer.

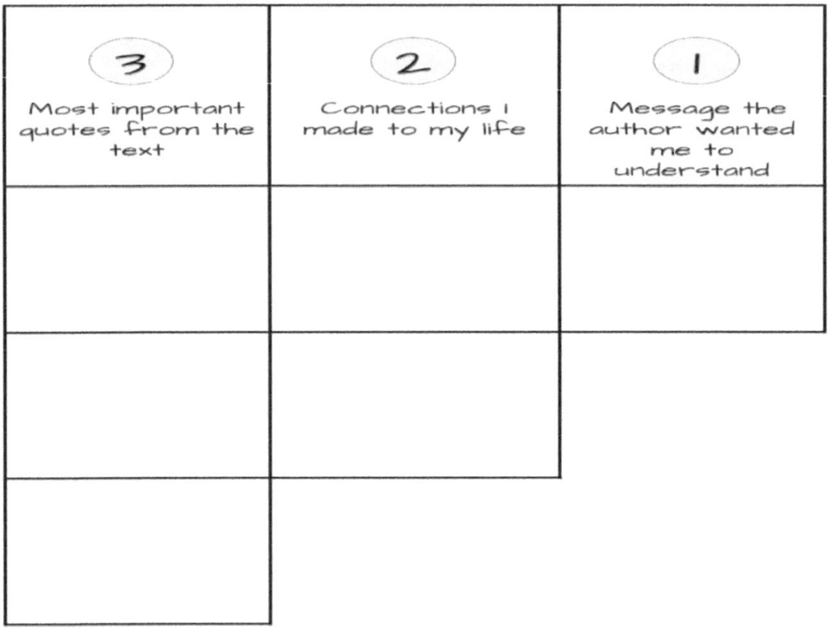

Figure 4.2 Example 3 2 1 Graphic Organizer.

CHALK TALK

Chalk Talk is a collaborative process where students are having conversations without talking. The teacher (or students) poses questions on the whiteboards or chart paper throughout the room. Students have time to ponder their thoughts and respond in writing or using visual responses. As they wander around the room, they can respond to each other, answer questions and draw lines and arrows to connect ideas, pushing their own and their peers' thinking forward (Brookfield, 2012; Ritchard et al., 2011). Resources for implementation of Chalk Talk can be found in the "Further Explorations" section in this chapter.

Because these ideas are short, they are easy to add into any classroom and can enhance learning and thinking in any classroom. These micro writing exercises can also be used as warm-ups or to generate ideas and directions for some of the writing projects shared in the remainder of the chapter. Consider your purposes and goals to determine which ideas would work best in your learning environment.

MULTIMEDIA PROCESS WRITING

Teaching students in the Information Age requires teachers to think outside of the box. For students to engage in all levels of learning, they must create something that does more than simply restate information. Multimedia process writing is one answer. Why use multimedia writing? In short—if multimedia is the format in which we receive information, we need to provide meaningful opportunities for students to analyze, evaluate, and create these same types of messages in a way that is authentic to themselves (Hobbs, 2011). If that isn't reason enough, consider students who are reluctant writers. Multimedia writing projects can capture students' interest who may not typically be enthralled with a traditional writing approach. The nature of these projects incorporates the world of sounds and images, in addition to the written word we are accustomed to.

> The technology and use of visuals appeal to many such students, and students who struggle with writing but are good at computers (or art) come to the project knowing they have some expertise—maybe even more than the teacher. This power can give them confidence that can carry through the writing. (Miller, 2007, p. 174)

So what is multimedia? At its core, media is defined as communication that can be categorized into four formats:

- Print (books, newspapers, magazines)
- Visual (movies, television, photographs, and drawings)
- Sounds (radio, recorded music, CDs, MP3 files)
- Digital (internet, email, video games, online social media) (Hobbs, 2011)

In short, media is the content that we all engage with daily. If the writing process and product are to be meaningful for students, the desired writing product should resemble the communication that is familiar to everyday life.

Robinson (2016) discusses several essential skills students require to be equipped for life beyond school. Robinson believes schools should facilitate the eight core competencies: curiosity, creativity, criticism, communication, collaboration, compassion, composure, and citizenship (Robinson, 2015). Through careful planning, teachers can provide students meaningful opportunities to develop each of these essential competencies by creating multimedia projects and the writing process.

What do these writing projects look like? While multimedia can take on countless formats, we will discuss a few that are stellar for the classroom setting. Among these are digital stories and public service announcements (PSAs).

The EDUCAUSE Learning Initiative defines digital storytelling as "the practice of combining narrative with digital content, including images, sound, and video, to create a short movie, typically with a strong emotional component" (Lynch, 2017, para. 1). Through the use of various technologies, students create a narrative, typically beginning with writing a script. Digital stories have a variety of uses in content area classes. They can be used for students to demonstrate their understanding of key historical or current events or to create stories that narrate their own experiences. For those who teach in the content areas, this particular format is especially beneficial in helping students understand humanities concepts (King, 2012). By creating digital stories to recount a specific event, students can celebrate nuances in their understanding through elements that are unique to this format, including music or images that contribute to a specific tone in ways that can be difficult to portray when limited to the use of words.

Although this format lends itself to creative and narrative writing, it is also valuable for depicting many science processes or concepts. Additionally, this format could even be used in mathematics, in which students could illustrate a given math concept or process. In either situation, the process will offer the students opportunities to continually refine their understanding while offering the teacher a clear demonstration of their learning.

In any application, a powerful component of this digital format is amplifying student voices (Lynch, 2017). This is especially true of students who may struggle with the English language and typically find difficulty fully demonstrating their learning through formal essays (consider ELL and ESE students who are developing their expressive English skills).

Remember Smokey Bear preventing wildfires? Or perhaps the Friends Don't Let Friends Drive Drunk campaign? PSAs are another stellar multimedia option that helps students think critically through the creation and writing process. A PSA is typically a short visual story that aims to bring awareness to a topic and usually includes a call to action (Ebert, 2019). Most of us are familiar with PSAs, even if we have never created one. Although PSAs may not always involve students in script-writing as with digital storytelling, this writing process requires students to create a persuasive story while exploring a selected topic they are passionate about. Circling back to Robinson and Aronica's (2016) critical elements, PSAs are a powerful tool to develop students' curiosity, creativity, compassion, citizenship, and communication. As with traditional writing projects, PSAs require students to consider their audience. Moreover, in this digital era, students have the potential for an authentic audience once their PSA is published.

MULTIGENRE/MULTIMODAL RESEARCH PROJECTS

Research papers have long been a mainstay in middle and high school classes throughout the content areas. Students learn about primary and secondary sources and how to correctly cite those sources—and why. Students move from subjective to objective writing stances, drawing on those outside sources for support for assertions made. They begin to understand the importance of evidence-based practices, data-informed practices—critical components of professions such as medicine and education. The best gift many of us received was having a teacher who explicitly taught the process of writing a research paper, a skill that applied through college. If you received that gift, seeing a research paper appear on a syllabus may not have filled you with joy, but not the anxiety those who'd never been taught the process of creating one experienced. Confidence born from a sense of competence does not necessarily lead to motivation or engagement with the academic task. Without both, academic achievement suffers (Irvin et al., 2007; Tate & Warschauer, 2018).

How do we marry motivation and engagement with the traditional research paper assignment? Enter the multigenre research project. According to Tom Romano (2000), the master of this alternative to the conventional research paper,

> A multigenre paper arises from research, experience, and imagination. . . . A multigenre paper is composed of many genres and subgenres, each piece self-contained, making a point of its own, yet connected by theme or topic and sometimes by language, images, and content. (Romano, 2000, pp. i–xi)

All the traditional elements and skills of mastering a research paper are present, but the genre or type of writing is not restricted to a more traditional research paper. In crafting a multigenre research project, student writers engage in rigorous work and stretch their writing muscles to represent information through various genres, including essays, poems, tweets, blog posts, and Instagram stories. And yes, a mini-research paper can be one of the genres. Multigenre evolves into multimodal when students include composing across an array of media. Students are now engaged in communicating a message beyond the single mode of a traditional research paper, to include combinations of text, images, video, and audio (University of Illinois, Springfield, 2021).

Romano (2000) collaborated with classroom teachers to create this compelling list of whys for multigenre research papers.

1. Students meet a multitude of standards in writing, research, reading, and vocabulary development.
2. Students learn how creativity and imagination are crucial components of interesting, thought-provoking research.
3. Students practice skills of grammar, usage, punctuation, and spelling. (Because multigenre kindles such excitement in students, they may be more inclined to take care in attending to the surface features of writing.)
4. Students practice skills of analysis and synthesis.

5. Students exercise multiple intelligences.
6. Students experience the exhilaration that comes with conducting inquiry fueled by a personal need to know and by the opportunity to communicate in multiple genres.
7. Students learn to be expansive in their writing.
8. Students experience the synergy of sharing ideas and accomplishments with community members who have similar goals.
9. Students experience agency as they shape and structure their papers and show what they know beyond teachers' expectations.

RESEARCH, EDITING, AGENCY, AND MOTIVATION

These are concerns of educators in all content areas. A history class is studying the Civil War. Multigenre papers as demonstrations of the learning involve students selecting genres appropriate to that era. Students begin crafting their own primary and secondary documents in the form of letters from soldiers to family members, journal entries, dispatches, and newspaper articles. Students in a freshman biology class create traditional lab reports and found data poems from their findings. Students examine their collected data with new eyes, reimagining and reorganizing the data in poetic form to add creativity to the communication of content knowledge. The process of creating the product with the infusion of student choice and creativity increases motivation and engagement, thus deepening student learning. Romano (2000) calls this "passionate immersion." Would we want any less for our students?

MORE MULTIGENRE SUPPORTS FOR CONTENT AREA WRITING AS SNAPSHOTS OF LEARNING

Support for students stretching their writing muscles while demonstrating their acquired content knowledge can also be found in perspective writing through role, audience, format, and topic (RAFT) prompts (Santa & Havens, 2008). RAFTs help students develop an awareness of the critical elements writers must consider when communicating to their reader and the questions they must address in crafting effective writing pieces:

- Role—Who are you as a writer? A Union soldier? A field biologist?
- Audience—To whom are you writing? A mayor? Yourself? CEO of a company?
- Format—In what format are you writing? A letter of complaint? A diary entry? A text message?

Table 4.1 Example RAFTS for Promised Land—The Grayson Family

Role: Who Are You as the Writer?	*Audience: To Whom Are You Writing?*	*Format: In What Format Are You Writing?*	*Topic (+Strong Verb):*
Andrew Jackson Grayson	Readers of a national newspaper	Letter to the editor	The challenges and benefits of moving west to California
Satanta, chief of the Kiowa	Children	Poem	How life is changing
An Exoduster in Nicodemus, Kansas	People who are thinking about moving to Kansas	FAQs (Frequency Asked Questions)	Questions and answers about life in Kansas
A child on a wagon train to California	A friend in the East	Personal letter	A description of the family's trip west on a wagon train
My Ideas			
Role:	**Audience:**	**Format:**	**Topic:**

Assignment—Create a character who has been affected by westward expansion. Write a text in the voice of your character. Use what you have learned from the map, artworks, primary sources, and other texts in this lesson to realistically portray how westward expansion has changed your character's life. Before you write, choose a RAFT for your writing. Below are some examples using the RAFT format. Then use the format to create your own project.

- Topic (+ strong verb)—What are you writing about? To alert consumers about the dangers of plastic in local waters? To request the replacement of a faulty product?

Include a visual image, and you provide students with additional support. Provide the support essential for English Language Learners and struggling writers, but make sure to include ones that will engage and challenge all students. An example from the Terra Foundation of American Art incorporating Jewett's *The Promised Land—The Grayson Family* (1850) is located in table 4.1.

The structure of the RAFT strategy helps teachers move from assigning to teaching, providing students with in-process support and a clear understanding of the assignment target they are aiming for.

WRITING AS DEMONSTRATION/ RESPONSE TO READING

"Why do we write so much if this is a reading class?" This student question voiced in a sixth-grade reading class is a reminder of how reading and writing are often presented as separate entities. Even the term *literacy*, which appears to be inclusive of both, is primarily synonymous with reading. My response to the student, "How will I know what you've learned in your reading if I don't have you write?" illustrates our central belief in reading and writing. The National Council of Teachers of English Policy Brief on Reading and Writing across the Curriculum states that

> discipline-based instruction in reading and writing enhances student achievement in all subjects. . . . Without strategies for reading course material and opportunities to write thoughtfully about it, students have difficulty mastering concepts. These literacy practices are firmly linked with both thinking and learning. (Fink, 2017, para. 3)

A few methods content area teachers can provide students with the opportunity to connect "reading course materials and writing thoughtfully about it" include the following:

The Minute Paper

The Minute Paper was developed initially by a physics professor to assess student knowledge following a class discussion or at the end of class; the Minute Paper can also be a method for assessing whether or not students are arriving in class having read the assigned text. The Minute Paper (so named as students are given 1 minute to complete the assignment) asks students to respond to the following questions: (1) What are the two (three, four, five) most significant (central, useful, meaningful, surprising, disturbing) things you have learned from the assigned readings? (2) What question(s) remain uppermost in your mind? (3) Is there anything you did not understand? The Minute Paper can also be a completely open response.

(STUDENT) QUESTION PROMPTS

Not surprisingly, most questions posed in classrooms are teacher generated, with students nearly always on the receiving/answering end. Flip this around. After discussing with students how questions are crafted (Question-Answer Relationships is an excellent tool), have students create single-sentence questions in response to an assigned reading. Next, have students exchange questions and provide text-supported responses.

ANNOTATIONS

First, no highlighters. Second, teach (meaning model) for students how to engage in active reading through the strategic marking. Active readers visualize, ask questions, make inferences, react when new information doesn't seem to "fit" with what they currently know. All should be reflected in marks as simple as symbols (? ! *). The more deeply and thoroughly students engage with and annotate the text, the more they demonstrate their knowledge from the reading. Step up student motivation by presenting creative annotation through simple illustrations representing reactions to the text. Add a digital element and present students with digital annotation tools available as apps. Have students discover new ones and share them with their classmates.

FURTHER EXPLORATIONS

- For detailed directions on the Boil It Down practice, visit https://taylormadeclassroom.com/2020/03/04/shrinking-notes-summary/.
- For descriptions of how to implement Chalk Talk and student work samples in multiple content areas, visit http://www.rcsthinkfromthemiddle.com/chalk-talk.html.
- This resource from teachwriting.org offers provides a How-To guide to help get started PSAs with PSAs: https://www.teachwriting.org/blog/2018/4/11/public-service-announcements-a-how-to-guide-for-teachers.
- This iSpring blog post offers valuable tips for using digital storytelling in the classroom. It includes sample projects with student guidelines, as well as sample published digital stories. https://www.ispringsolutions.com/blog/5-digital-storytelling-assignments-in-the-classroom.
- For an example RAFT activity, with ideas for how to generate an effective RAFT, visit https://www.terraamericanart.org/tools-for-teachers/raft-writing-strategies/.

REFERENCES

Anderson, L. W., Krathwohl, D. R., Airasian, P. W., Cruikshank, K. A., Mayer, R. E., Pintrich, P. R., Raths, J., & Wittrock, M. C. (2001). *A taxonomy for learning, teaching, and assessing: A revision of Bloom's Taxonomy of Educational Objectives*. Longman.

Banks, S. R. (2012). *Classroom assessment: Issues and practices* (2nd ed.). Waveland Press.

Bereiter, C., & Scardamalia, M. (1996). Rethinking learning. In D.R. Olson & N. Torrance (Eds.), *The Handbook of education and human development: New models of learning, teaching and schooling* (pp. 485–513). Basil Blackwell.

Bloom, B. S., Englehart, M. D., Furst, E. J., Hill, W. H., & Krathwohl, D. R. (1956). *Taxonomy of educational objectives, Handbook I: The cognitive domain*. McKay.

Brookfield, S. D. (2012). *Teaching for critical thinking: Tools and techniques to help students question their assumptions*. Jossey-Bass.

Brookfield, S. D. (2015). *The skillful teacher: On technique, trust and responsiveness in the classroom* (3rd ed.) Jossey-Bass.

Christopher, B. (2018). Micro writing is having a macro impact on identity development. Appendix of *Stories of change: Educators shift practices to reach all learners*. EdSurge Research.

Ebert, W. (2019). Public service announcements: A how-to guide for teachers. https://tinyurl.com/pb5hvdyr.

Ferlazzo, L. (2018). Micro-writing for English learners. *Educational Leadership, 75*(7). http://www.ascd.org/publications/educational_leadership/apr18/vol75/num07/Micro-Writing_for_English_Learners.aspx.

Fink, L. (2017). *The relationship between reading and writing*. https://ncte.org/blog/2017/12/relationship-writing-reading/.

Graham, S. (2019). Changing how writing is taught. *Review of Research in Education. Sage Journals, 43*(1), 277–303. https://doi.org/10.3102/0091732X18821125.

Graves, D. H. (2002). *Testing is not teaching: What should count in education*. Heinemann.

Hobbs, R. (2011). *Digital and media literacy: Connecting culture and classroom*. Corwin.

Irvin, J. L., Meltzer, J., & Dukes, M. (2007). *Taking action on adolescent literacy: An implementation guide for school leaders*. ASCD.

King, M. D. (2012). Digital storytelling: Digital storytelling combines cross-content literacies and technology to make the humanities come alive for today's students. *Principal Leadership, 13*(2), 36. https://link.gale.com/apps/doc/A380748039/PROF?u=sain11218&sid=PROF&xid=4471db37.

Kittle, P. (2008). *Write beside them: Risk, voice, and clarity in high school writing*. Heinemann.

Lynch, M. (2017). How digital storytelling can amplify your students' voices. https://tinyurl.com/4asay3mn.

Miller, L. (2007). Space to imagine digital storytelling. In T. Newkirk & R. Kent (Eds.), *Teaching the neglected "R"* (pp. 172–185). Heinemann.

National Commission on Writing. (2003). The neglected "R": The need for a writing revolution. College Board. https://archive.nwp.org/cs/public/print/resource/2523.

Rich, J. (July 1, 2014). Six word memoirs in the classroom. International Literacy Association. https://literacyworldwide.org/blog/literacy-now/2014/07/01/six-word-memoirs-in-the-classroom.

Ritchart, R., Church, M., & Morrison, K. (2011). *Making thinking visible: How to promote engagement, understanding and independence for all learners*. Jossey-Bass.

Rief, L. (2018). *The quickwrite handbook: Mentor texts to jumpstart your students' thinking and writing*. Heinemann.

Robinson, K., Ph.D., & Aronica, L. (2016). *Creative schools: The grassroots revolution that's transforming education*. Penguin Books.

Romano, T. (2000). *Blending genre, altering style: Writing multigenre papers.* Boynton.

Selfe, C. L. (2007). *Multimodal composition: Resources for teachers*. Hampton Press.

Romano, T. (n.d.). What multigenre does for students. http://www.users.miamioh.edu/romanots/assignments/what%20MG%20Does%20for%20Students.doc.

Santa, C. M., Havens, L. T., & Valdes, B. J. (2004). *Creating independence through student-owned strategies* (3rd ed.). Kendall/Hunt.

Shelby-Caffey, C., Úbéda, E., & Jenkins, B. (2014). Digital storytelling revisited: An educator's use of an innovative literacy practice. *The Reading Teacher*, *68*(3), 191–199. 10.1002/trtr.1273.

Tan S. C., Hung D., & Scardamalia, M. (2006) Education in the knowledge age: Engaging learners through knowledge building. In D. Hung & M. S. Khine (Eds.), *Engaged learning with emerging technologies* (pp. 91–106). Dordrecht: Springer.

University of Illinois, Springfield (2021). What is multimodal? Center for Academic Success. https://www.uis.edu/cas/thelearninghub/writing/handouts/rhetorical-concepts/what-is-multimodal/.

Chapter 5

Note-Taking versus Note-MAKING!

Carolyn E. Graham and Carrie Fallon-Johnson

After years in the classroom at all levels—primary, intermediate, middle, and high school—one thing has continued to ring true—students who write about the content which they are learning makes a tremendous impact on building long-term knowledge and skills across academic courses (Daniels et al., 2007). Writing is not just for the language arts classroom! The acts of listening to and viewing lessons, practicing skills, writing, and discussing essential information, and applying the new content are the basic components of learning new skills. These actions also promote the retention of those skills and allow for them to be built upon over time (Daniels et al., 2007).

Unfortunately, we have found that the skill of note-taking has become more of a performative act rather than a skill that is refined and revisited to embed learning. Note-taking as a strategy for studying and acquiring information is stuck in some old-school or even antiquated styles within our buildings. We surveyed our colleagues about the note-taking practices in the middle and high schools where we teach. Based on the survey responses, we found that notes taken are generally not reviewed in the classroom, and notes are often graded for completeness with notebook checks—they are not regularly revised or discussed after the lesson to influence retention for understanding and analysis over time. Alas, notes taken by students are done so by copying what is said by the teacher or from what is written on the board or in a presentation—colleagues shared that "If I write it, they write it" or that students are cued "this is IMPORTANT so write it down." The majority of those surveyed shared that when they provide note-taking structures, they are some form of guided, mostly cloze-style notes. Those same teachers only half believe that the notes that they share are effective for all the students in their courses. If we, as educators, are doing the work to get course content and skills to students through the task of note-taking then it is time we take this typical classroom task to the next level. It is time for a shift in doing and thinking in the classroom when it comes to writing notes.

Before we dive in, experiment with these doodle notes (Danziger, 2014) created via the Canva website (Canva, 2021). Fill in the first two boxes in the graphic organizer below (see figure 5.1). You can record any ideas or notes in the remaining margins using words or images as you read through this chapter.

Notes, note-taking, and note-making can seem like a detached concept rather than a vehicle to embed learning and acquire standards mastery. Standards, by design, are functionally mastered when new information is connected to previously acquired skills. Teachers of all content area need to explicitly teach a variety of ways to take notes, allow time for learners to revise those notes by planning for class discussions and note revisions with peers, and ultimately letting their students choose the most effective way for collecting information after a variety of options have been shared and practiced. The note-making skill will ensure students can continue to transfer this skill to all content areas and become lifelong learners possessing the tools to embed their own learning. Learners who feel that they have ownership of this information and can attain this information in the ways that make the most sense for them will then be able to complete the entire cycle of learning (Sulla, 2015). Teachers who

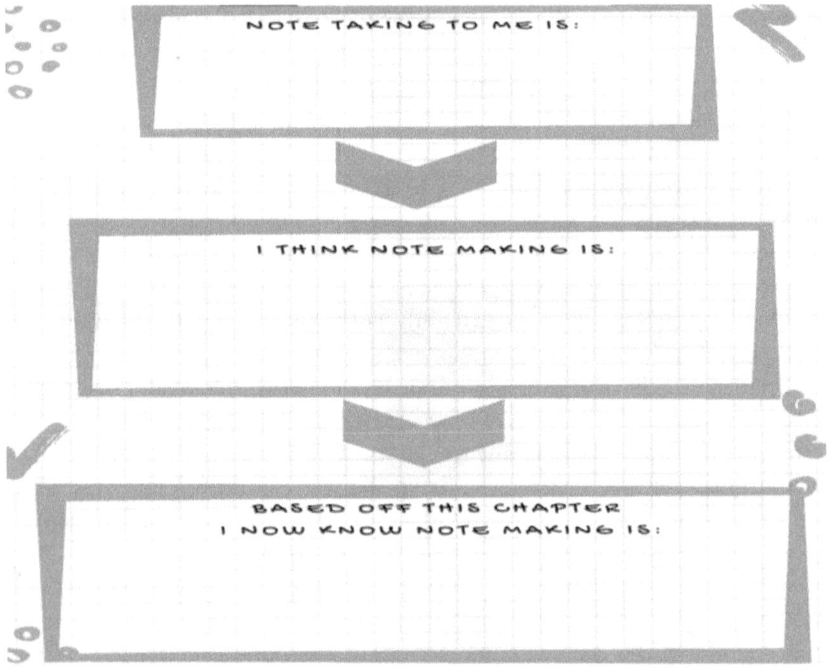

Figure 5.1 Note-Taking versus Note-Making.

include a variety of options for students to gain new knowledge within the classroom show that they truly understand how note-taking is a key to unlocking a lifelong learner. Providing students with options for collecting information and allowing for opportunities to revise and fine-tune that information is the shift where note-taking becomes the more valuable skill of note-making.

EFFECTIVE NOTE-TAKING IN THE LEARNING CYCLE

As soon as students hear, "take out some pen and paper for notes," the groan is audible, and the resistance is palpable. A lot of this resistance in general seems to be because either:

A) students do not really know *how* to take notes
B) students do not understand *why* we take notes
C) students are sure the whole process will suck out their life force for the day.

And as we mentioned earlier, if the process of note-taking is never revisited it reinforces the confusion around the purpose of the notes and ends up seeming like 'busy work.' We are constantly engaging in a battle with students' past experiences with note-taking when working to introduce the skill to them in a way and manner they will be enthusiastic to engage in. But what happens when we take something dreaded, like the age-old "death by PowerPoint Note Taking" and add rigor and ownership to transform the strategy into note-making?

Author, researcher, and storyteller Brene Brown (2017) wrote, "Creativity embeds knowledge so that it can become practice. We move what we are learning from our heads to our hearts through our hands. We are born makers, and creativity is the ultimate act of integration—it is how we fold our experiences into our being" (p. 17). So how do we get students to that creation stage especially when addressing new concepts and new content? We know that working with our hands and creating is what helps to embed learning. How do we get to the creation phase of learning faster and without students becoming disengaged? This is where the concept of note-taking shifts into note-making. This distinction of the "taking" to the "making" represents a shift in onus of content from the teacher, being the 'sage on the stage—deliverer of all knowledge,' to students becoming the meaning makers and facilitators of their own knowledge.

MAKING THE NOTES WORK

The research has shown that effective note-taking improves test scores for students. The primary indicators of the student-produced notes being effective in the cycle of learning are collaboration and the opportunity for revision to the notes students take (Luo et al., 2016). This process begins with whichever medium students select to take notes, whether it be Cornell Notes, Sketchnotes, or anything in between. It continues by taking a pause to trade with a peer, discuss, and collaborate on the notes which will result in a revision to the original notes to make them more effective. A revisit and revision step in the note-taking process also provides students with another guided session using the content that students need to learn to demonstrate mastery of the concepts and skills. Creating a collaborative model of note-taking also builds a communal responsibility and understanding that students are in the learning process and cycle together. This shift in the traditional method of lecture/solo notes can alleviate the boredom and dread commonly associated with note-taking—it makes the process a community effort and offers several opportunities to discuss, revise, and solidify understanding of the required content.

As educators, we know that taking notes and applying study skills are necessary parts of learning. We see this in reference to Kolb's Learning Cycle, the process of not only note-taking but note-making reflects multiple stages in the learning cycle. Depending on the style of notes students use, they can cycle through Kolb's Learning Cycle in a note-making session (McLeod, 2017). This starts with, according to Kolb's theory, a concrete experience, where new information or ideas would be expressed to the student through various forms. This leads to the second part of the learning cycle which is the reflective observation of the new experience. After students have the concrete experience of reading or listening to new information, they will reflect on what needs to be included in their notes. The third phase in Kolb's Learning Cycle is abstract conceptualization, in this phase students can synthesize new learning with old learning or modify their old thinking considering the new information. This is what researchers have shown is missing with simply copying from a lecture or digital presentation. The last phase of Kolb's Learning Cycle is active experimentation where the learner applies all the newly gained knowledge to the world around them.

Carousel Notes

An example of this shift in note-taking to note-making, as well as Kolb's Learning Cycle, is evident in the strategy of Carousel Notes. This note-taking strategy makes students the creators and facilitators of new knowledge rather than just short-term receptacles of content. It creates an interdependency to help ensure engagement as well as knowledge acquisition. This strategy is best used with foundational concepts and definitions (see figure 5.2).

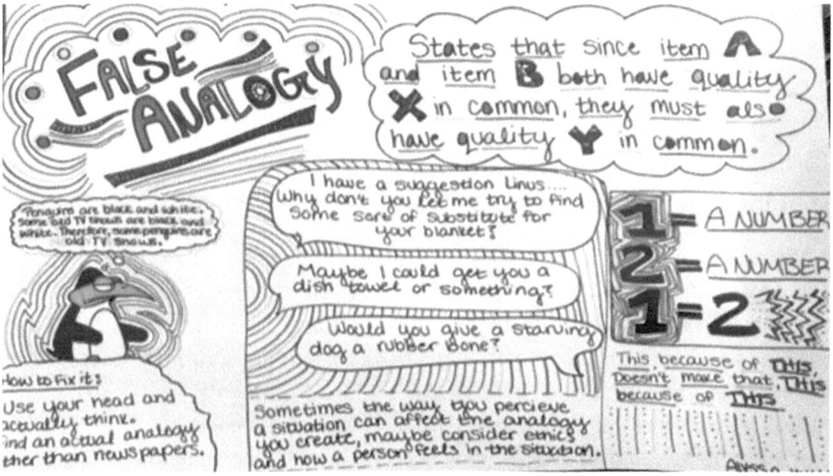

Figure 5.2 Example of Carousal Notes Poster.

Carousel Notes can be defined as a hybrid of two well-known strategies, the jigsaw strategy (Hance, 2017) and a gallery walk (Mason, 2021). Students are assigned a specific term or concept to build a poster around. They are the owner and the expert of that content and provide the knowledge for the poster they create. They will then display their poster in the classroom. The class will then take a gallery walk to read, view, and record all the content into their own notes or a graphic organizer. This can also be done digitally through a variety of web-based platforms such as Padlet or Thinglink.

If we view this strategy considering Kolb's Learning Cycle (McLeod, 2017) to better understand how note-taking can shift to note-taking, it would look like this. Students use class time to create these posters based on their own knowledge as well as research they conduct to find examples and images to explain the concept or content they are assigned. This part of the assignment reflects step two of the learning cycle by providing a reflective observation in the form of a definition in their own words and seeking out other examples. The next day the students' posters are hung around the room to create a carousel or gallery walk of learning. This gallery walk reflects phase three of Kolb's learning cycle since it requires students to create abstract conceptualizations since they are then responsible for recording the definition or concept as well as examples from each of their peers' posters. As a conclusion to the note-making process and to conclude Kolb's Learning Cycle, students engage in a class discussion about their notes and observations of the concepts or content they recorded and why. During this process, they can also revise their notes based on this discussion. We know audiences check out after about 10 minutes, but you can keep grabbing them back by telling narratives or creating events rich in emotion (Medina, 2018) so to create that experience that imbeds learning this strategy uses creation, repetition, physical movement, emotions, and application to real life, as well as reinforcing learning through Kolb's Learning Cycle.

Doodle Notes

Another example of a note-making strategy that works to embed learning and have students extend knowledge into the synthesis and creation phase of learning is through a strategy called doodle notes (Math Giraffe, 2014). It is the idea of integrating both sides of the brain to record and then embed knowledge (see figure 5.3).

In the simplest of terms, this strategy has students take notes on new concepts, ideas, definitions, or material and then take that new knowledge and create a visual representation of it. This big idea can be seen throughout multiple strategies across content areas. In an English course, for example, students need to know certain vocabulary terms used in graphic novels to deeply understand how the concepts of theme and symbolism are presented in the text. For students to embed this knowledge, doodle notes allow students to take those vocabulary terms and represent them visually via their own mini

Figure 5.3 Doodle Notes. Example of doodle notes.

graphic novel page. It can have a story or just be as simple as a visual representation of the terms that demonstrates understanding.

Again, in this example, we can see note-taking shift into note-making. Students take specific content knowledge and vocabulary words (concrete experience), plan how to reflect their meaning in a comic of their own (reflective observation), then create their own comic to embed their meaning into their memory (abstract conceptualization). They then sharing their comics with their table group and even the whole class, which while it can feel scary, is a form of abstract experimentation to see if they got the definitions and applications correct as well as completing the learning cycle.

AVID One Pager Strategy

Another similar strategy is the AVID One Pager Strategy (Potash, 2021). When this strategy is applied to specific concepts like theme, setting, characterization, or even broader concepts across the curriculum, it can be an amazing creation-based strategy to have students make and record their learning. While not considered traditional notes, when learning in this manner, students can embed and retain more knowledge and ideas than with traditional note-taking methods.

HIGH TECH VERSUS LOW TECH

The twenty-first-century learner is expected to be well versed in content, hardware, and software to acquire content, practice skills, and produce in the learning environment. Teachers and curriculum writers work to develop lessons and activities for their students and often consider the "SAMR Model." This model was devised and revised by Dr. Ruben R. Puentedura as a means for educators to understand the integration of technology into the everyday classroom. Note-taking with technology generally falls into the first two categories of SAMR—Substitution and Augmentation in which technology enhances the activity but is not transforming it in ways that otherwise could not be done with other resources (Puentedura, 2018). When educators and students use technology to substitute or replace a traditional activity like completing guided notes or worksheets with a digital version, this is called Substitution. Educators and students use Augmentation to replace the traditional activity with some functional improvements, for instance, completing notes in an online notebook and adding images or links to other sources to support the content. Many students have their own devices and some schools are able to provide devices for students to participate in daily digital activities in the classroom. With access to so much technology in schools, is taking notes on a device more beneficial for the student than using the traditional pencil and paper? Well, that depends on how digital note-taking is taught by the teacher and is able to be produced by the student.

We live in a fast-paced and ever-changing world. Teachers do increasingly more in the classroom in the same amount of time that has been provided for decades. Teachers and students have more options and more technology at their fingertips than ever before. Writing is slow work. It requires more effort on the learner's part and more time planned for by the teacher. Writing in a traditional manner is also proven to support learning content far more than word processing does. Researchers Pam Mueller and Daniel Oppenheimer (2014) observed and collected data on students who handwrote their notes and those who typed them in the same courses. Mueller and Oppenheimer found that students who wrote their notes had far fewer words on the page and often had incomplete sentences and some doodles; students who typed had more words, more complete sentences, and often had copied what they heard or saw verbatim. In their study, the researchers also tested their subjects' memory for factual details from the courses' content, their conceptual understanding of the material, and their ability to synthesize and generalize the information (Mueller & Oppenheimer, 2014). Students who handwrote their notes had a stronger conceptual understanding of the material than those who typed their notes, and the writers were better able to apply and integrate the content. They understood the content better and were able to do more with it. The researchers tested their hypothesis three times, and all three times students who handwrote notes scored better on their various assessments.

Such results do not mean that technology is ineffective for note-taking or note-making, they just mean that the right technology needs to be utilized for effective learning to take place. Whether you follow the ideas of "visual note-taking" (Pillars, 2016) or "sketchnoting" (Rohde, 2013), the right technology can bridge the twenty-first-century gap between the traditional wide-ruled notebook and the newest iPad or Chromebook. These educators show how everything that a student can do with pencils, markers, and foldable inserts, they can also effectively do with the right App and a stylus—writing by hand with a device is just as effective as paper and pencil. It is also easier than using a pencil for the avid stylus user!

Sketchnotes

Sketchnotes can be created by anyone, anytime, anywhere—the technology comes in after the notes are made to share and sections are highlighted for review and analysis. Revisiting the notes is essential, so repeated access to the product and feedback from peers needs to be scheduled and encouraged (Rohde, 2013) to complete the learning cycle.

Edusketching

Visual note-taking or "edusketching" is a process that begins as a collaborative effort between the educator and learner, and it must include pictures or images. Using visuals can enhance the concept retention and understanding for certain learning styles, improve learning by 55 percent, and support English Language Learners and students with varying abilities (Pillars, 2016). This style of note-taking uses both sides of the brain with pen movement, creation or addition of images, and discussion of key elements to small details. Apps or software for devices such as iPad Pro or and two-in-one devices can be used to create and enhance visual notes while using a stylus, fingertip, or inserted graphics. However, students and educators need to remember these are notes! The details and concepts included in the notes, peer discussions, references to and revisions of notes over time, and sharing for feedback all fortify and solidify the learning process of any new information (Pillars, 2016).

PLANNING FOR NOTE-MAKING

Here is a quick guide to support you with planning for and applying note-making in your classroom. Your options are endless, but your choices must be intentional. Students need to be explicitly taught a variety of note-taking strategies before they should be allowed to create their own notes. When note-taking, the end in mind is that notes are a mechanism for reinforcing information for the long term, not just passing the quiz at the end of the semester.

Know your students—their needs, accommodations, learning styles, strengths, and gifts. While choosing strategies to collect and refine ideas and concepts in your classroom, be sure to always consider your students first. Once a variety of structures have been implemented, then it is time to give your students the choice of which note-taking tools to use. Always schedule time for discussion, review, and revision—this cannot fall on your students' shoulders if note-taking is to be an effective learning tool. Plan all parts of the learning cycle before assessing your learners. Those results will help prove whether your students are note-taking or note-making.

To embed your new learning from this chapter, go back to your doodle notes which you created while reading. Revisit what you thought note-making would be. Then upon reflection, revise your notes to reflect your new learning and new knowledge acquired about the intentional shift educators should take from note-taking to note-making to best serve their learners. Share your ideas and fine-tune your own thinking. Now, you have the tools to

Table 5.1 Note-Making Strategies at a Glance

	Description	*Low Tech*	*High Tech*	*Differentiation*
Cornell Notes	Two-column notes	Paper/pencil with a template or student created	Digital in One Note or Google Classroom	Templates, Cloze Notes, fill in the blank, premade questions
Category or Coded Notes	Annotations through codes and symbols	Key provided and students mark up a printed text or document	Done online through Perusall, One Note, Google Classroom, hypoth.is	Provide the code, jigsaw the text
Class Notebooks	Interactive notebook with templates and anchor charts	Preprinted pages, composition notebooks	Canvas, One Note, Google Classroom, Seesaw	Small groups, partner work, Cloze Notes, transcripts provided for lecture
Collaborative Notes	Jigsaw content and concepts for students to share their portion	Posters, small groups, Think-Pair-Share	Padlet, Thinglink	Cloze notes provided; content provided
Outline Notes	Format of identifying topics, main ideas, and details	Student created in notebooks or on paper while reading, listening, or viewing	Student created in digital notebooks or on documents	Provide the outline headings and students complete the details
Sketchnotes	Using images (such as doodles, diagrams, or graphics) with written notes to record information	Pencil, paper, colored writing utensils	Digitally create what you would on paper with a device and stylus using apps like Notability, Inkflow, and Procreate	Should be taught and practiced with structure provided
Input/Output	"Input" is the important information, facts, data, and definitions. "Output" is the student's thoughts, ideas, opinions	Left side is input and right side is used for output; entire notebook is utilized to complete the structure	Columns created in MS Notebook or Google Classroom; a document for MS Word or Google Docs is created to create the structure	Teacher-created outlines for input and output as guided notes

plan and support your students with becoming note-MAKERS in any course and lifelong learners with the tools to own and embed their learning.

REFERENCES

Brown, B. (2017). *Rising strong: How the ability to reset transforms the way we live, love, parent, and lead.* Random House.

Daniels, H., Zemelman, S., & Steineke, N. (2007). *Content-area writing: Every teacher's guide*. Heinemann.

Danziger, B. (2014). *About.* Doodle Notes for Education. http://www.doodlenotes.org/about.html.

Design Anything. (2021, May 17). Canva. https://www.canva.com/.

Hance, M. (2021, January 19). *The jigsaw method teaching strategy*. TeachHUB. https://www.teachhub.com/teaching-strategies/2016/10/the-jigsaw-method-teaching-strategy/.

Luo, L., Kiewra, K. A. & Samuelson, L. (2016). Revising lecture notes: How revision, pauses, and partners affect note taking and achievement. *Instructional Science, 44*(1), 45–67. https://doi.org/10.1007/s11251-016-9370-4.

Mason, J. (2021, May 12). *Gallery Walk*. BetterLesson. https://betterlesson.com/strategy/13/gallery-walk.

McLeod, S. A. (2017, October 24). *Kolb—learning styles and experiential learning cycle*. Simply Psychology.

Mueller, P. A., & Oppenheimer, D. M. (2014). The pen is mightier than the keyboard. *Psychological Science*, *25*(6), 1159–1168. https://doi.org/10.1177/0956797614524581.

Pillars, W. (2016). *Visual note-taking for educators: A teacher's guide to student creativity*. W.W. Norton & Company.

Pillars, W. (2017). *4 domains of visual note taking*. Ms. Wendi's World. https://3.bp.blogspot.com/-_fJhOkLdbuw/WXapOnNuxEI/AAAAAAAAMX4/j__1fotynowy9cREGplYVT653uVmS8VKQCLcBGAs/s1600/4DomainsSketch.JPG.

Potash, B. (2021, April 29). *A simple trick for success with one-pagers*. Cult of Pedagogy. https://www.cultofpedagogy.com/one-pagers/.

Puentedura, R. R. (2018, September 28). *SAMR and TPCK: A hands-on approach to classroom practice*. Ruben R. Puentedura's Blog. http://hippasus.com/blog/archives/425.

Rohde, M. (2013). *The sketchnote handbook: Illustrated guide to visual notetaking*. Peachpit Press.

Sulla, N. (2015). *Students taking charge: Inside the learner-active, technology-infused classroom*. Routledge.

Chapter 6

Springboards for Writing in Mathematics

Christine Picot

TO BEGIN

Think about your very own classroom. The goal of teaching mathematics to secondary students is now a reality. You begin to plan your first lesson within the unit of instruction. As you review the teacher edition for guidance, you encounter the following word problem suggested for instruction. Solve this problem.

1. Mr. Morris likes to watch the Packers play football. There are sixteen football games a season, and each game lasts for about 3 hours. How many hours does Mr. Morris spend watching the packers for the whole season?

Did you come up with 48 hours? If so, great. If not, what did you do wrong? How would you know the computational errors if students were to solve this problem to address misconceptions? Now consider the same problem with a few edits. Solve this problem.

2. Mr. Morris likes to watch the Packers play football. There are sixteen football games a season, and each game lasts for about 3 hours. How many hours does Mr. Morris spend watching the packers for the whole season? Write to explain your solution process.

Would you find the first or the second problem more beneficial from an instructional standpoint? Reflect on why you chose your answer.

If you are reading this chapter, you might have two different areas of thought. If I'm a math teacher, why do I have to teach writing? Or, I have heard of mathematical literacy but am not quite sure what that means for me as a math teacher. As a district mathematics coach, I had many teachers express these thoughts too. During my fifteen years of coaching and mentoring teachers, an analysis of student data was always a key indicator of where I needed to focus my support. Interestingly, a common theme emerged time and time again, word problems or prompts. Students were experiencing a difficult time solving the word problems, and more often than not, those pesky snips of complex text often required students to write. They were to write their solution process, describe their reasoning, or prove their answer. Often textbooks have word problems embedded to integrate the real-world application of concepts taught through computation. However, the teacher's edition provided limited support and, at times, none at all. Additionally, there is a heavy focus on word problems in high-stakes assessments. This, too, increases pressure for teachers to integrate these prompts as often as possible. Furthermore, high-stakes assessments will have designated areas for students to compose short or extended responses directly connected to the mathematics prompt. Consider prompt in figure 6.1 from the National Assessment of Educational Progress (2017).

Word problems can be a challenge for teachers and students due to the complexity of mathematics when embedded in a linguistic format. You, too, may have also agonized when it was time to solve these types of problems. A study conducted by Joseph (2012) reviewed the academic language in word problems in student textbooks and noted that more than 50 percent of the wording within the prompt of the average word problem was composed of academic vocabulary. For example, symbols and domain-specific academic vocabulary (math words) can make mathematics a language of its own; it is no wonder word problems can be difficult! However, these prompts are helpful to demonstrate conceptual understanding and provide perfect opportunities for teachers to assess understanding formatively. Within word problems, the students have to comprehend the problem more often and write a response by explaining a process or justifying a solution. All of these processes make the use of the skill of writing a necessity in learning mathematics and communicating mathematically.

> Richard wants to estimate the average (mean) monthly temperature of the United States last year. He will choose one of the following methods to do this.
>
> Method 1: Richard selects his state and nine other states that are near his state. He finds the average (mean) monthly temperature of each of these 10 states and uses these numbers to compute the average monthly temperature of the United States.
>
> Method 2: Richard selects 10 states by writing the names of all 50 states on cards, with one state's name on each card. Then he places all the cards in a hat and takes out 10 cards without looking. Finally, he finds the average (mean) monthly temperature of each of these 10 states and uses those numbers to compute the average monthly temperature of the United States.
>
> Which method is better, method 1 or 2? Explain why.
>
> (Question ID:2013-8M6 #13 M141601)

Figure 6.1 National Association of Educational Progress Prompt.

Within this chapter, I will take you through my journey with mathematics teachers and the resources we have utilized that have proven to increase student growth and achievement in some of the lowest-performing schools I served—all through the integration of writing. To attain mathematical literacy, this chapter will explore several facets of writing in the mathematics classroom. Standards emphasizing the importance of higher-order thinking skills supported by writing will assist the reader in the importance of standards-based instruction aligned to mathematical communication. There are many cognitive benefits reported in mathematics connected to writing and solidifying conceptual understanding. Additionally, the type of mathematical prompts that facilitate a constructed response will be investigated. Aligned to the type of prompt, the format for writing through journals provides ideas for instructional tools to support writing. Textbooks and their role in the mathematics classroom will assist teachers in utilizing the textbook prompt to plan for writing. Finally, the mathematics writing planning guide will help to support teachers in making instructional decisions of how and when to teach writing in the mathematics block. I will also provide you with practical applications of how to integrate writing in the mathematics classroom, from planning to strategies for instruction with a focus on word problems. More importantly, I will provide you with the knowledge of why writing is a helpful tool to facilitate conceptual understanding of mathematics to build mathematically literate students.

A VIGNETTE

As a district mathematics coach, my planning sessions with teachers focused on how to increase student achievement whether during small group or whole-class instruction. During my conversations, I began to understand that teachers were struggling with the integration of mathematics literacy. Teachers wanted students to utilize mathematics vocabulary during discussions in both oral and written form. They also wanted students to not only acquire the content but also retain the knowledge. Additionally, they wanted students to feel confident in reading mathematics word problems and solving them. Moreover, the textbook lacked the support needed to plan for word problem instruction. We began to analyze the types of word problems and create our own aligned to the content. We also integrated whiteboard applications, such as *ShowMe*, to digitally create a word problem and explain through writing their solution process. We made sure each student had a spiral notebook or a math journal to solve problems and write down the solution steps and processes. Interestingly, every activity we developed within multiple grade levels incorporated writing. After some time, students became comfortable with writing, and teachers demonstrated confidence embedding writing within their instruction. Academic vocabulary was utilized more than ever in the classroom. After reflecting on my experiences providing teacher support, I began to understand that my coaching philosophy for teachers was centered on the process standard of communication, more specifically, that of writing.

IMPORTANCE OF COMMUNICATING MATHEMATICALLY

In order to achieve mathematical literacy, the process skill of communication in both oral and written form is encouraged in the mathematics classroom (NCTM, 2000). The act of writing in the mathematics classroom provides benefits in both teaching and learning. For example, writing can facilitate the learning of mathematics content by providing a "window" into students' thinking so teachers can plan targeted instruction by analyzing student responses (Herbel-Eisenmann, 2007). Having students problem-solve while focusing on their mathematical thinking process also facilitated higher-order thinking skills such as metacognition (Sowder, 2007). Furthermore, the acquisition of domain-specific vocabulary and opportunities to facilitate conversations through writing integrates both fields of language arts and mathematics organically (Burns, 2004; Pugalee, 2005). Miller (1991) observed, "students who will not ask questions in class may express their confusion privately in writing" (p. x).

ORAL DISCUSSIONS AND MATHEMATICS WRITING

As noted, writing in mathematics has many benefits. Additionally, writing can serve as a catalyst for oral discourse. During my conversations with teachers, it was noted that students were able to communicate more efficiently during discussions because of writing. A simple, turn and talk or think pair share about your prompt provided students with the confidence and vocabulary needed to share their work with other students.

There are many benefits that writing encapsulates related to oral discussions. Writing can be used as a catalyst to facilitate conversations whereby students can verbalize their responses by thinking about how they worked out solutions, organized their responses, evaluated their own approaches, and clarified their thinking while drawing upon prior knowledge for conceptual development (Steele, 2001, 2005). The teacher's role was not only to ask students questions but the teacher was also an active listener who provided formative insight when planning based on students' predications and algebraic ideas. In addition to the many benefits of communicating mathematically, mathematics standards also highlight the importance of integrating writing to solidify conceptual understanding.

MATHEMATICS AND STANDARDS

Mathematical standards developed by various organizations underscore the importance of utilizing mathematical processes to help students acquire mathematics content. For example, the NCTM (2000) identified five process standards for teachers to follow when teaching mathematics content. Similarly, the NRC formulated the strands of mathematical proficiency (NRC, 2001), standards that highlight the processes students should encounter while learning mathematics content. Furthermore, members of the Council of Chief State School Officers (CCSSO) and the National Governors Association Center for Best Practices developed common standards and mathematical practices for all states (CCSSO, 2010) that support the acquisition of specific processes to attain mathematics proficiency. A comparison of these processes suggests particular skills support critical thinking and problem-solving. Moreover, the process of reasoning is central in achieving mathematics proficiency (CCSSO, 2010; NCTM, 2000, 2006, 2011).

To facilitate mathematical reasoning, many of the process standards and mathematical proficiency standards suggest that students justify their mathematical solutions through speaking and writing. Writing is encouraged to facilitate conceptual development (Nuckles et al., 2020, 2010; Bicer et al., 2018). Furthermore, writing in many forms is considered an essential fixture for learning content across disciplines (Graham et al., 2020; Bazerman, 2009; Boscolo, 2008). Writing-to-learn (WTL), another writing-focused educational initiative encourages instructors to leverage writing to support students as they uncover content, make connections with prior knowledge, and unearth new ideas and understandings through the writing process (Nagin, 2003). Furthermore, writing has been noted to improve metacognitive skills and facilitate reflection (Brewster & Klump, 2004).

COGNITIVE BENEFITS OF WRITING IN MATHEMATICS

In the mathematics classroom, to promote students' conceptual understanding of the content acquired, writing is encouraged to explain a solution process, justify a strategy, or communicate reasoning (Urquhart, 2009; Vygotsky, 1962).

In addition, writing in mathematics can help students acquire the domain-specific vocabulary needed to communicate mathematically (Beck et al., 2002; Fisher & Frey, 2008; Graves, 2009; Marzano & Pickering, 2005).

There are many cognitive benefits reported through writing in mathematics. Through the National Writing Project, Nagin (2003) noted that writing is considered a tool for thinking while emphasizing how the facilitation of such instruction can foster active learning and significant reflection. More specifically, "writing could be a complex activity; not just a skill or talent, it's a method of inquiry and expression for learning in all grades and disciplines" (p. 3). Writing in journals can impact learning from a metacognitive stance by supporting the monitoring of comprehension and evaluation of learning outcomes (Nuckles et al., 2010).

Higher-order thinking processes have also been noted as a benefit to writing in the mathematics classroom. Schema building and metacognition were reported to occur during the act of mathematical writing. For example, Pugalee (2001) noted that a metacognitive framework was present in students' written analysis of algebraic mathematical prompts. Furthermore, the use of thinking through reflective prompts assisted in building schema knowledge through identification, elaboration, planning, and executing of information (Steele, 2001, 2005).

Teachers can also use students' writing to identify strengths and gaps in students' content knowledge and understand students' affective positions and feelings about mathematics content (Urquhart, 2009; Romberger, 2000). As noted, writing in mathematics is a valuable tool. Writing facilitates cognitive processes needed to compose a response while attending to the language of the prompt.

MATHEMATICAL WRITING PROMPTS

Within my coaching and mentoring of teachers, we explored the different types of mathematics prompts that assist in facilitating a constructed response. For this chapter, the term prompts refers to items (problem solvers, story problems, and word problems) that require student responses in written form. Within our exploration, we found that there are several different types of prompts located in curricula materials.

TYPES OF WRITING PROMPTS

Within the field of mathematics, there are four types of mathematics writing prompts. These types of prompts are (1) content, (2) process, (3) affective, and (4) narrative prompts (Baxter et al., 2001; Dougherty, 1996; Shield & Galbraith, 1998). According to Urquhart (2009), a mathematics content prompt focuses on mathematical concepts and relationships. Student responses can be in the form of defining, comparing and contrasting, and explaining (Dougherty, 1996). As defined by Urquhart (2009), the following is an example of a content prompt.

- How do you know 1/4 is greater than 1/5? Explain your thinking.

Dougherty (1996) noted that when students respond to why various solution strategies or steps were used to solve a problem, this would be defined as a process prompt. Because of the language of justification, the following can be labeled as a process type prompt.

- How can you justify your solution to the volume of this shape?

A prompt in which students express their opinions about mathematical content or feelings is an affective prompt (Baxter et al., 2001; Shield & Galbraith, 1998). An example of an affective prompt in mathematics would be the following.

- Which types of problems do you prefer to solve, geometric problems or algebraic problems, and why?

The last type of writing prompt in mathematics is the narrative prompt. This type of prompt is commonly seen on high stakes assessments and in creative writing. Within this type of prompt, the constructed response can be in the form that portrays math content in an imaginary or real-world sense. Furthermore, narrative content and themes are embedded within children's literature (Burns, 2004; Whitin & Whitin, 2000). The following math prompt was noted by Burns (2004) to facilitate a story construction. This type of prompt was coded as a narrative type in the framework:

- Write a story entitled, "If I were a pirate!" Be sure to discuss your treasure map using the coordinate systems and how you would ensure a "secret" hiding place for your treasure.

The Mathematical Task Force (2017) reported that students can write for different reasons so it is important to use various types of prompts to assist in communicating and reasoning in mathematics. For example, exploratory prompts are described as students personally making sense of the content through a problem, situation, or one's ideas. Additionally, describing or explaining a process is known as writing to inform or explain. Students can also write to construct or critique an argument based on a mathematical content or processes. Furthermore, content, process, narrative, and affective prompts align with what the task force notes as mathematically creative. Mathematically, creative writing posits the documentation of original ideas, problems, or solutions; conveys fluency and flexibility in thinking; and elaboration of mathematical, conceptual understanding (Casa et al., 2017).

During my work with teachers, we began to select prompts from the mathematics textbooks aligned to prompt types. After analyzing the type, we engaged in a workshop where teachers would edit the prompt based on the type of prompt they wanted their students to solve. We engaged in this work because some of the prompts were limited to multiple-choice selection, one-word response, or simple computation and required no justification or reasoning connection. These simple edits required students to reflect more critically about the content within the problem, explain a solution process, develop a story, or describe a feeling. For example, notice the additional sections added in italics to the sample textbook problem in table 6.1.

As you will note, teachers made several iterations aligned to the original textbook problem. Teachers pointed out that it was "fun" creating these problems. Teachers also found it beneficial to think about how students will write their responses to these prompts. Using this method of instruction, teachers noted how students' responses would provide insight into students' conceptual understanding and misconceptions. In Professional Learning Communities (PLCs), teachers planned, shared, and utilized the journal prompts within their mathematics instruction.

Table 6.1 Textbook Problem Revision

Original Problem	If the area of a circle is 81 square feet, find its circumference.
Process Prompt	If the area of a circle is 81 square feet, find its circumference. *What steps did you perform to solve this problem? Write those steps in order.*
Content Prompt	If the area of a circle is 81 square feet, find its circumference. *How do you know your answer is correct?*
Narrative Prompt	*Write about a time you were a tailor for a King, and he needed a new crown. However, you made a mistake in calculating the circumference! What happened as a result? How did you solve this problem? Be sure to include specific calculations of area and circumference in your story.*
Affective Prompt	*What do you like solving better the area or circumference of a circle and why?*

JOURNALS AND MATHEMATICAL WRITING

Math journals are a conducive format for facilitating writing in the mathematics classroom based upon the objective and prompt. Students can describe solution processes, justify their thinking, write a math story, or describe feelings and attitudes toward a specific concept. Baxter et al. (2001) noted the benefits of journals in a mathematics classroom as a tool to reinforce mathematics concepts by describing or explaining mathematical ideas or reasoning. The journal can be utilized and accessed as a tool for mathematical thinking and referenced throughout the year to aid in retention and to acquire pertinent vocabulary (Monroe & Panchyshyn, 1995).

Mathematical writing prompts for journaling can be developed by teachers. As an example, Baxter et al. (2005) examined how writing revealed students' mathematical proficiency. The questions were geared toward identifying what writing in mathematics revealed as students were encouraged to write about their mathematical ideas and reasoning by utilizing teacher-developed writing prompts. The findings suggest that writing was a way to communicate their feelings. In contrast, the teacher's writing responses provided valuable information regarding students' mathematical proficiency and assisted with targeted planning for mathematics lessons centered upon student understanding.

Powell (1997) also found journals to be a valuable tool in the mathematics classroom. An additional classroom study analyzed responses in journals related to the Greatest Common Factor and the Least Common Multiple. The findings suggested that journaling captured the verbal representation of students' thinking. Journaling provided the teacher a way to capture, examine, and respond to students' mathematical thinking. In this study, journaling allowed students to reflect on mathematical experiences, examine their written reflections, and reflect on their ideas critically. This type of reflective thinking enabled the students to become active learners. Through journaling in these case studies, the researcher noted that writing helped the students develop confidence in their understanding of mathematics and become more thoroughly engaged with mathematics.

TEXTBOOKS AND PLANNING FOR MATHEMATICAL WRITING

To support writing in the mathematics classroom, mathematic textbooks contain nonconventional problems such as project tasks and open-ended problems (Fan et al., 2013). Because writing requires the detailed description of thought (Vygotsky, 1978), written responses are intended to develop students' abilities to reason and develop mathematical thinking and acquire content knowledge (Bicer et al., 2013; Nuckles et al., 2010).

The mathematics textbook is an essential component in mathematics instruction and has been researched as a dominant tool within the mathematics classroom (Hagarty & Pepin, 2002; Johansson, 2005; Malzahn, 2002). However, due to the pervasiveness of the textbook as a predictor of mathematics instruction, Joseph (2012) explored the support within teacher's editions related to mathematics writing prompts and noted the challenges connected to the mathematics textbook teacher edition as a guide to facilitate writing prompts in mathematics instruction. Through developing an analytic framework, mathematical writing prompts were coded by the support provided in the teacher's edition. The findings indicated that limited support in the teacher's edition left the instructional planning and implementation of the writing prompt to teachers' discretion. This may pose several issues as beginning teachers, who are novices in mathematics planning, may resort to textbooks specifically for guidance. Furthermore, teachers familiar with best practices in literacy instruction may also default to the teacher's edition for support utilizing these types of prompts.

The following section will present writing in mathematics framework designed for instructional planning of mathematics prompts found in the textbook or composed. This framework is structured to assist teachers in planning for writing in mathematics and will assist in filling the gap within instructional planning and delivery. The *Mathematics Prompt Instructional Resource Guide (M-PIRG) framework* has been utilized and modified as a planning guide in K–12 classrooms for planning and writing in mathematics (Picot & Schneider, 2021, p. 23).

INSTRUCTIONAL RESOURCE GUIDE (IRG)

Due to the limited support in mathematics textbooks for the planning and teaching of mathematical writing, the IRG was developed based on an action research design that analyzed how teachers plan for writing in the mathematics classroom (see table 6.2). A sampling of in-service teachers (n=35) during PLC meetings indicated varied objectives within the mathematics block for teaching writing in mathematics. Based on common themes within analyzed conversations, the categories of Objective of Instruction, Method of Instruction, Type of Prompt, Delivery of Instruction, and Assessment were noted as salient points within instructional planning, therefore utilized as categories in the M-PIRG.

According to the M-PIRG, the Objective of Instruction states that writing can have an instructional objective in five different areas. If your aim is to

Table 6.2 Mathematics Prompt Instructional Resource Guide (M-PIRG)

Objective	*Method*	*Type of Prompt*	*Delivery*	*Assessment*
Introduce *upcoming objectives* through student interviews and analysis of student data.	Formative Assessment	Prompt encompasses *upcoming standards.*	Whole Group Small Group Independent	Formative Rubric Learning Scales (Not graded)
Practice mathematics content, vocabulary, and strategies of *previous objectives.*	Warm-Up/Review	Prompt encompasses *review of previous standards*	Whole Group Small Group Independent	Formative or Summative (Grading Optional)
Instruct mathematics content, vocabulary, and strategy of *current objective.*	Introduction of Content	Prompt *introduces upcoming standard.*	Whole Group Small Group	Formative (Rubric Optional/Not graded)
Practice content, vocabulary, and application of strategies of *current objective.*	Practice of Content	Prompt encompasses *practice within the current standard.*	Whole Group Small Group Independent	Formative (Rubric Optional/Not graded)
Assess the mastery of mathematics skills/concepts taught within the *current objective.*	Summative Assessment	Prompt encompasses *previously taught standards. (Can use same Formative Assessment prompt).*	Whole Group Small Group Independent	Formative or Summative (Rubric/Graded)

understand what students know about a specific concept before you begin planning for instruction, planning appropriately targeted instruction to areas of misconceptions or limited understanding, then the format for writing would be Formative Assessment. If your objective is to assess growth at the end of an instructional unit, then the format for writing would be Summative Assessment. Therefore, the same prompt from the Formative Assessment can be administered again at the end of the unit to determine mastery and growth as a Summative Assessment. If your objective is to have students get their "math brains" warmed up, then a writing prompt from previous instruction to reinforce acquired concepts, the format for writing would be Warm-Up. If your objective is to have students practice a real-world application word problem to reinforce computational methods, your writing format would be Practice of Content. However, some teachers choose to use WTL-specific concepts to construct meaning, utilize vocabulary, and develop strategies, then the format for writing would be Introduction of Content.

When interviewed, some teachers utilized the objective and planned for one prompt a week. Others would choose two or three objectives using the various formats aligned to the M-PIRG. For example, some teachers utilized the Formative Assessment prompt again as a Summative Assessment to plan appropriate intervention groups. While some teachers found that the M-PIRG provided an appropriate instructional sequence and used each objective from Formative Assessment "directionally" downward to Summative Assessment on the framework. Teaching a word problem through each writing objective was noted to provide a valid instructional sequence in the mathematics block. Those teachers reported that this instructional sequence allowed for additional writing beyond what was previously instructed before the M-PIRG was implemented.

The Standards of Mathematical Practice describe varieties of expertise that mathematics educators at all levels should seek to develop in their students. These practices rest on important "processes and proficiencies" with long-standing importance in mathematics education. The first of these are the NCTM Process Standards of Problem Solving, Reasoning and Proof, Communication, Representation, and Connections. Second are the strands of mathematical proficiency specified in the National Research Council's report *Adding It Up*: adaptive reasoning, strategic competence, conceptual understanding (comprehension of mathematical concepts, operations, and relations), procedural fluency (skill in carrying out procedures flexibly, accurately, efficiently, and appropriately), and productive disposition (habitual inclination to see mathematics as sensible, practical, and worthwhile, coupled with a belief in diligence and one's own efficacy). These eight practices describe the thinking processes, habits of mind, and dispositions that students need to develop a deep, flexible, and enduring understanding of mathematics—the true goal of mathematics teaching and learning. Through my work with teachers, I have uncovered that purposeful planning and developing appropriate and engaging prompts, the two fields of literacy and mathematics, come together organically, creating mathematically literate students.

REFERENCES

Baxter, J. A., Woodward, J., & Olson, D. (2005). Writing in mathematics: An alternative form of communication for academically low-achieving students. *Learning Disabilities Research & Practice, 20*(2), 119–135.

Baxter, J. A., Woodward, J., & Olson, D. (2001). Effects of reform-based mathematics instruction in five third grade classrooms. *Elementary School Journal, l01*, 529–548.

Bazerman, C. (Ed.). (2008). *Handbook of research on writing: History, society, school, individual text.* Lawrence Erlbaum.

Bicer, A., Capraro, R., & Capraro, M. (2013). Integrating writing into mathematics classrooms to increase students' problem solving skills. *International Online Journal of Educational Sciences, 5*(2), 361–369.

Beck, I. L., McKeown, M. G., & Kucan, L. (2002). *Bringing words to life: Robust vocabulary instruction.* Guilford Press.

Bicer, A., Perihan, C., & Lee, Y. (2018). The impact of writing practices on students' mathematical attainment. *International Electronic Journal of Mathematics Education, 13*(3), 305–313. https://doi.org/10.12973/iejme/3922.

Boscolo, P. (2008) Writing in primary school. In C. Bazer (Ed.), *Handbook of research on writing: History, society, school, individual, text* (pp. 293–309). Erlbaum.

Brewster, C., & Klump, J. (2004). *Writing-to-learn, learning to write: Revisiting writing across the curriculum in Northwest secondary schools.* Northwest Regional Educational Laboratory.

Burns, M. (2004). Writing in math. *Educational Leadership, 10,* 30–33.

Casa, T. M., Firmender, J. M., Cahill, J., Cardetti, F., Choppin, J. M., Cohen, J., & Zawodniak, R. (2016). Types of and purposes for elementary mathematical writing: Task force recommendations. http://mathwriting.education.uconn.edu.

Dougherty, B. (1996). The write way: A look at journal writing in first-year algebra. *The Mathematics Teacher, 89*(7), 556–560.

Fan, L., Jones, K., Wang, J., & Xu, B. (Eds.) (2013). Textbook research in mathematics education. ZDM—*The International Journal on Mathematics Education, 45*(5).

Fisher, D., & Frey, N. (2008). *Word wise and content rich, grades 7–12: Five essential steps to teaching academic vocabulary.* Heinemann.

Graham, S., Kiuhara, S. A., & MacKay, M. (2020). The effects of writing on learning in science, social studies, and mathematics: A meta-analysis. *Review of Educational Research, 90*(2), 179–226. https://doi.org/10.3102/0034654320914744.

Graves, M. F. (1986). Vocabulary learning and instruction. In E.Z. Rothkopf (Ed.), *Review of research in education, 13* (pp. 49–90). American Educational Research Association.

Haggarty, L., & Pepin, B. (2002). An investigation of mathematics textbooks and their use in English, French and German classrooms: Who gets an opportunity to learn what? *British Educational Research Journal, 28*(4), 567–590.

Herbel-Eisenmann, B. (2007). From intended curriculum to written curriculum: Examining the "voice" of a mathematics textbook. *Journal for Research in Mathematics Education, 38*(4), 344–369.

Johansson, M. (2005). The mathematics textbook: From artifact to instrument. *Nordic Studies in Mathematics Education, Nomad, 10*(3–4), 43–64.

Joseph (Picot), C. (2012). Communication and academic vocabulary in mathematics: A content analysis of prompts eliciting written responses in two elementary mathematics textbooks (Doctoral dissertation). http://scholarcommons.usf. edu/etd/4344/.

Malzahn, K. A. (2002, December). Status of elementary school mathematics teaching (Report from the 2000 National Survey of Science and Mathematics Education). Horizon Research. http://2000survey.horizonresearch.com/reports/#statusteaching.

Marzano, R. R., & Pickering, D. J. (2005). *Building academic vocabulary: Teacher's manual.* Association for Supervision and Curriculum Development.

Miller, L. (1991). Writing-to-learn mathematics. *Mathematics Teacher, 84*(7), 516–521.

Monroe, E. E., & Panchyshyn, R. (1995). Vocabulary considerations for teaching mathematics. *Childhood Education, 72*(2), 80–83.

National Council of Teachers of Mathematics. (2000). *Principles and standards for school mathematics.* Author.

National Council of Teachers of Mathematics. (2006). *Curriculum focal points for prekindergarten through grade 8 mathematics.* Author.

National Council of Teachers of Mathematics. (2011). Common core state standards joint statement. http://www.nctm.org/standards/content.aspx?id=26088.

Nagin, C. (2003). *Because writing matters: improving student writing in our schools.* Jossey Bass.

National Governors Association Center for Best Practices & Council of Chief State School Officers. (2010). Common Core State Standards. Authors.

National Research Council (2001). Adding it up: Helping children learn mathematics. In J. Kilpatrick, J. Swafford & B. Findell (Eds.), *Mathematics learning study committee, center for education, division of behavioral and social sciences and education.* National Academy Press.

Nuckles, M., Hubner, S., Dumer, S., & Renkl, A. (2010). Expertise reversal effects in writing-to-learn. *Instructional Science: An International Journal of the Learning Sciences 38*(3), 237–258.

Nückles, M., Roelle, J., Glogger-Frey, I., Waldeyer, J., & Renkl, A. (2020). The self-regulation-view in writing-to-learn: Using journal writing to optimize cognitive load in self-regulated learning. *Educational Psychology Review.* https://doi.org/10.1007/s10648-020-09541-1.

Picot, C. J., & Schneider, J. J. (in press). Word problems in the mathematics textbook: An instructional resource guide to support writing instruction. *FAMTE Transformations*.

Powell, A. (1997). Capturing, examining, and responding to mathematical thinking through writing. *The Clearing House, 71*, 21–25.

Pugalee, D. (2001). Writing, mathematics, and metacognition: Looking for connections through students' work in mathematical problem solving. *School Science and Mathematics, 101*(5), 236–243.

Pugalee, D.K. (2005). A comparison of verbal and written descriptions of students' problem-solving processes. *Educational Studies in Mathematics, 55*, 27–47.

Romberger, J. (2000). Writing across the curriculum and writing in the disciplines. Purdue OWL. http://owl.english.purdue.edu/handouts/WAC.

Shield, M., & Galbraith, P. (1998). The analysis of student expository writing in mathematics. *Educational Studies in Mathematics, 36*(1), 29–52.

Steele, D. (2001). Using sociocultural theory to teach mathematics: A Vygotskian perspective. *School Science and Mathematics, 101*(8), 401–416.

Steele, D. (2005). Using writing to access students' schemata knowledge for algebraic thinking. *School Science and Mathematics, 105*(3), 142–154.

Sowder, J. T. (2007). The mathematics education and development of teachers. In F.K. Lester (Ed.), *Second handbook of research on mathematics teaching and learning* (pp. 157–223). National Council of Teacher of Mathematics.

Urquhart, V. (2009). *Using writing in mathematics to deepen student learning*. McREL.

U.S. Department of Education Institute of Education Sciences. (2017). National Assessment of Educational Progress. The Nations Report Card Sample Questions. IES National Center for Educational Statistics https://www.nationsreportcard.gov/math_2017/sample-questions/?grade=8.

Vygotsky, L. S. (1962). *Thought and language*. MIT Press.

Vygotsky, L. S. (1978). *Mind in society: The development of higher psychological processes*. Harvard University Press.

Whitin, D. & Whitin, P. (2000). Exploring mathematics through talking and writing. In M.J. Burke & F.R. Curcio (Eds.), *Learning mathematics for a new century* (pp. 213–222). National Council of Teachers of Mathematics.

Chapter 7

Writing to Support Science Learning and Success

Laura Altfeld and Cheryl Berry

ANECDOTAL EVIDENCE

As you embark on your journey as a science instructor, you will be challenged to meet your students' varied needs and demands to write like scientists and use writing itself to learn science. Throughout this chapter, we will introduce you to essential strategies, tools, and the rationales for their uses in your future or current classrooms. Consider the following anecdote from one of our authors who employs several of these tools in her classroom to get you started. Enjoy!

VIGNETTE

The bell rings, the corridor to my classroom will be flooded with students in less than a minute. Soon I will have seventh-grade students meandering through rows of desks to find their assigned spot and then look at me inquisitively as they wonder what will be the lesson of the day. But, of course, I don't have to read their minds because, as preteens, they frequently and openly say what is on it, "Science class should be fun!" or the absolute rabble-rousers ask, "Can we blow something up today?" Today I don't have to speak a word to settle them down. I stand at the front of the class with ten packs of different bubble gums sitting on the table in front of me. Of course, I was bombarded with questions as they entered, asking if they get to chew the gum, and I smile and wait in silence. This is a technique I often use to quiet the students when I know I have something they want to know about because they will quiet each other down, saving me the work.

I then tell them we will Predict, Observe, and Explain (POE) today and instruct that they get out their science journals to write about our exploration of the physical properties of gum. I am still passively commanding quick compliance about the impending writing because they still want to know about the fate of the gum. I put the students in groups of three and ask them what pack (brand and flavor) of bubble gum their group wants. I then explain to the students they each get a piece of bubble gum from the pack to unwrap and observe. I tell them to unwrap the gum and write what they observe and predict using all their senses. I suggest they consider size, color, shape, texture, weight, odor, taste, and overall appeal of the gum but do not limit any description as there must be at least six traits described. I then ask students to predict how each feature will change after they chew the piece of gum and write this prediction down. I get the anticipated comments "Ewww" or "I don't look at my gum after I chew it, I just spit it out."

After students make their predictions, I invite the students to chew their gum and share their predictions with their group members as they enjoy their gum. After ample chewing and talking time, I ask students to put their gum back on the wrapper and write their observations. What changed about the gum? Again, students share their observations, and then I choose one student from each group to share the group responses with the class. I focus on one characteristic, the weight (really mass) of the gum. No one suggested a change in mass. I ask about this, and the students are perplexed as they declared the same piece of gum went in and then out of their mouth. I suggest we use the scales to take the mass of the unchewed gum in their packs and compare it to the mass of their chewed gum. Again, what do they predict? Will they have the same mass or will mass increase or decrease after chewing it. After students use the scales to quantify the gum pre- and postchewing mass, they write their observations.

Students are then told to explain the results in writing: explain why mass did not change, why it increased, or why it decreased, thus completing the POE writing outline. We then share results as a class, with the aha moments being the students' realization of a mass change in the gum due to sugar loss.

The inquiry activity in the above vignette was a lesson opener that relied on writing, using the POE outline, to help students make sense of scientific Predictions, Observations, and Explanations, and explore the concept of mass through the instructional approach of Activity Before Concept (ABC) using a science journal. The activity also leverages the benefits of integrating discrepant events in science inquiry. Discrepant events are demonstrations that have outcomes not immediately predicted by students. These events scaffold learning by students recognizing their misconceptions and motivation to replace them with an evidence-based explanation (Longfield, 2009).

The students all get a piece of wrapped gum to take with them, and even though they promise not to chew the gum in another teacher's classroom, I fully anticipate complaints from other teachers during bus duty at dismissal time. As for the next lesson, we will explore mass and density together with the same ABC, POE journal writing, and discrepant event strategies, this time, it will be soda instead of gum. What will happen when I put a can of diet soda and regular soda in a bucket of water? Will they both sink or float? I guess you will have to come to my class to find out.

CONTENT AREA VERSUS DISCIPLINARY LITERACY

The term content area literacy is often used to refer to reading and writing in history, math, and science courses. However, it employs reading and writing strategies common to all disciplines. Typically, content area literacy is modeled by teachers during instruction and practiced by students in class assignments, according to the International Literacy Association (2017). By contrast, disciplinary literacy necessitates a specific emphasis on the reading and writing norms that uniquely define an academic discipline and are not common practice in other disciplines (International Literacy Association, 2017).

So, what are those norms that uniquely define writing in the sciences? The practice of science is undertaken by individuals who follow the scientific method as they explore and investigate the natural world, ultimately seeking to accurately describe, understand, and share their findings with others.

The process of scientific writing enables scientists to document, elaborate on, and convey information about nature. Perhaps most often, scientists write to themselves, as when recording observations and data and establishing hypotheses that attempt to explain observed patterns and events. In this case, detailed and descriptive writing helps the investigator recall the specifics of observations after time has passed, supporting reflection on them later with new insight (Turner & Broemmel, 2011). At other times, and arguably, more importantly, scientists are writing for audiences to persuade others of their knowledge and value within a given community (including classrooms). Reporting accurately and in a detailed but shared systematic manner enables ease of interpretation by other scientists and supports the understanding and replicating work important for disciplinary progress (Turner & Broemmel, 2011). In all cases, science writing is expected to utilize the terminology, common knowledge, voice (active vs. passive), perspective (first vs. third), and citation style norms of a given scientific subdiscipline.

WHAT IS SCIENCE LITERACY?

The National Academy of Sciences (1996) defines science literacy as the ability to explain natural phenomena, evaluate the validity of claims, make evidence-based informed decisions, and evaluate the types of evidence presented in an argument. The emphasis on evidence-based information is key, as is the understanding of naturally occurring phenomena. Science literacy is enhanced when teachers keep science topics conceptual, relatable, and interactive. Teachers must make science "modern" and "socially relevant" (Hobson, 2000), with discussion topics chosen for their relatedness to real-world occurrences within students' daily lives. Grant and Lapp (2011) identified the following four elements as essential to teaching science literacy. One, topics used to learn science concepts and objectives should be connected to the students' real-life experiences and current events. Two, engage students in reading material on science topics from varied viewpoints, including scientific research. Three, model the way scientists read and write to fortify student understanding of evidence-based text. And four, provide differing data to students for their evaluation, either collected by themselves or from outside sources.

SCIENCE WRITING BENEFITS STUDENTS

Why do students need to know how to read and write in science? According to Singletary and Sampson (2011), the following are three key reasons science literacy is vital to students. First, science literacy emphasizes evidence-based writing. This is an important skill for students to differentiate between academic, fiction, nonfiction, and persuasive writing genres as lifelong learners. Second, students need scientific literacy to understand scientific issues and make educated and informed decisions as members of society. And third, science literacy enables students to use critical thinking skills to interpret and understand models, theories, and patterns more easily.

LEARNING THEORIES

The true power of learning theories is wielded when a teacher selects the best traits from multiple theories and uses these traits effectively in combination with one another. Theories contributing to the framework for science writing include behaviorism, constructivism, and social learning theories.

One of the critical assumptions of the behaviorism theory (Skinner, 1937) is that repetition and reinforcement are essential to the learning process

(Merriam & Caffarella, 1999). Novice writers will discover that the science writing process is iterative. It requires them to adapt their existing perceptions of writing formats and conventions to those needed for the science discipline based on feedback from their teacher and peers. Becoming a skilled writer in science requires repetition and reinforcement of the correct writing formats and conventions supported by positive outcomes or feedback. The teacher can reinforce behaviorism by providing timely feedback on writing exercises, discouraging repetition of incorrect writing conventions, rewarding effort, praising good science writing, and setting up positive writing activities that promote the desired writing behavior.

Bruner's (1966) constructivist theory of learning is, according to McLeod (2019), a learning method in which students get to be active participants while their learning is scaffolded over time. Bruner's approach holds the teacher as a critical component of constructivist learning because the teacher is responsible for choosing the appropriate writing activities for students to participate in to construct their own meaning from science over time through the writing process. According to Bruner's constructivist approach to learning (a form of cognitivism), when an educator aids a learner to recognize what they know about a concept and link it to new information, learning about that concept progresses. The use of constructivism in science writing embraces the nature of scientific inquiry and encourages students to write with the goal of learning science in mind. When used in science writing, the goal of constructivism is the active construction of meaning from science concepts rather than the passive absorption of it (Clark, 2010).

The social learning theory is like the constructivist theory in that it supports collaborative group work in science writing. People are information processors and learn from watching those performing similar behaviors in their environment. Cognitive processes are at work while watching others because people do not simply mimic behaviors but instead process the need to repeat the modeled behaviors based on observed outcomes (McLeod, 2016). Such observations and cognitive processing are essential to learning the format and conventions of science writing. Students learn from both reading and evaluating the scientific writing of other students and peer-reviewed scientific literature. Self-efficacy is the learner's perception of their ability to manage situations that may include novel or unpredictable elements (Bandura, 1977). As a learner's self-efficacy increases, so do confidence and success in science writing. Having learners set writing goals, tracking their writing progress, and use carefully selected writing models can aid in student's self-regulation of the writing process.

Learning theories are essential frameworks for science writing instruction because they inform teachers about how students create new meaning and construct knowledge. However, there is no theoretical framework that works every time for every science writer; each has its benefits and limitations. The selection of traits from learning theories is based on the learners' needs and constraints of the learning environment. Therefore, science teachers must assess all students' writing abilities and select writing activities considering both the benefits and limitations of the theories supporting those activities and differentiate according to the needs of the individual learner. For example, suppose timely feedback from the teacher is impossible for a writing activity as required for the behaviorism theory. In that case, constructivism or social learning theories should be considered, allowing for increased peer interaction instead of teacher contact.

WRITING-TO-LEARN SCIENCE

Embedding writing activities in science instruction will maximize students' learning within the science discipline. A science writing activity should have an authentic purpose and motivate students to write (Dlugokienski & Sampson, 2008). The following are authentic and motivating science writing activities to engage your students in writing-to-learn science. Any of these can be used as formative or summative assessments based on the desired instructional goals.

Freewriting

Popularized by Peter Elbow in *Writing without Teachers* (1973), freewriting is a practice that has students put pen to paper (or fingers to keyboard) and write continuously, without stopping, for a given period established by the instructor. The writing can be in response to a prompt or not, again, as set by the instructor. Freewriting is solely for the author and, therefore, is uncensored; it is done with zero regard for spelling, punctuation, grammar, or structure of any sort. Hence, the value of freewriting is not in the polished nature of the product but, instead, the attention it brings to the goings-on of the author's mind. Done at any point during a class session, freewriting allows students an opportunity to warm up and focus their attention and intention mentally. Thus, it can be an excellent pre- and postsession activity in a science class, bringing to light any unexpected gaps, misunderstandings, biases, or insights about a particular concept or mechanism.

Journal Writing

"Writing is thinking. That's what I tell my students," says Dannell Stevens of Portland State University, "They think it's what's done after they think"

(Rhem, 2009). Journaling, when used effectively, offers a trove of benefits for students to use to deepen their learning. The keys to effective journaling, Stevens offered, are to provide students with various journaling activities, show them that there are surprises to be found in their writings, and submit not their journals but, instead, reflections on their journal entries. Journaling can also incorporate freewriting as a technique. Breaking away from the need to craft a structured entry opens the door for using the journal in a more accessible and creative way. Providing students with in-class and out-of-class journal entry time prompts and requirements varies the use of the journal, enabling more diverse recordings of their thoughts. Further, and perhaps most importantly, students can be required to reflect on their entries by, for example, rereading what they have previously written and writing a summary of those thoughts and that experience. This reflection becomes a valuable metacognitive activity where new discoveries of personal insight and learning can be made.

Refutational Writing

Refutational writing is a form of persuasive writing to help students learn science, and, according to Dlugokienski and Sampson (2008), it can be found in three different formats. One form involves a one-sided presentation of evidence to persuade the reader to accept the writer's theory. A second form consists of the creation of a two-sided nonrefutational display of two sides of an event. It often indirectly leads the reader to the writer's theory through favoritism of evidence toward one side. And the third form involves the intentional favoring of one side using evidence while also discrediting the other side. An example of a refutational writing assignment, described by Dlugokienski and Sampson (2008), is to provide a theory and then ask the student to provide evidence to refute the view to make the presented proof more compelling than the original explanation given to the student. The theory can be a concept or something observable. An example provided by Dlugokienski and Sampson (2008) suggested to students that most people think water droplets get on the outside of a glass of drinking water because it seeps through the glass from the inside to the outside. Students are challenged to refute this statement with compelling evidence.

Writing Probes and Prompts

Brown (2019) recommends coupling the "Explore before Explain" approach to science activities with assessment probes to leverage students' prior knowledge and experiences to contextualize new knowledge about science events and motivate students to use evidence to explain those events in writing.

Assessment probes are formative assessments used during instruction to gauge students' understanding and can be as simple as giving the students 2 minutes to answer a question at the start or end of class. Brown (2019) gave the example of a lesson on heat transfer, beginning with an assessment probe asking students to identify in writing the direction of heat transfer between ice and lemonade in a glass. Students must also include in their written response an explanation for their answer. This activity is then followed up with an "Explore before Explain" activity, including a demonstration of both a cold water flask and hot water flask with different color dyes being placed into a tub of cold water and observing the movement of the water in both flasks. Upon observing the event, students explain the direction of heat transfer using evidence from their observation. After students have explored the concept of heat transfer through the assessment probe and demonstration, they are given time to discuss their findings with other students without any direct instruction from the teacher. Then the teacher provides the scientific explanation and addresses any lingering misconceptions about the science concept.

Brown (2019) asserted the following sequencing of instruction (embedded in the "Explore before Explain" approach) maximizes student learning and can all be presented in writing. First, prior knowledge and lived experiences are activated. Second, interaction and personal experience with the data are related to the concept. Third, the data allows for the formation of real evidence to support explanations. And finally, direct instruction related to the idea is connected to the students' constructed explanation of the concept.

"ABC" and "POE" prompts work well as science lesson openers or activating strategies that require students to construct their science knowledge by connecting what they observe and what they think those observations mean in their writing. The ABC approach is similar to the "Explore before Explain" approach but leaves options for differing levels of exploration within the activity and may not necessitate a hands-on inquiry approach as typically found in the "Explore before Explain" model. The POE science writing can be a formative assessment similar to the assessment probe but does not pose a question. Instead, it requires students to brainstorm a prediction (P) about what will happen before an activity/demonstration/experiment takes place, write their observations (O), and explain (E) what they observed. The student explanation becomes the formative assessment and can be used as the springboard into the teacher's direct instruction on the concept, concluding the ABC model.

"Argument-Driven Inquiry" (ADI) is an instructional probe that requires students to explain the scientific phenomenon under investigation, provide evidence to support their explanation, and provide their reasoning as to why the evidence provided lends support to their explanation. The unique features of this model include student argumentation of their evidence, a double-blind peer-review process, and the inclusion of all forms of science literacy by requiring students to engage in science reading, writing, and verbal communication skills (Sampson et al., 2009). The following are the steps of the ADI instructional model as provided by Sampson et al. (2009), emphasizing writing. First, a science phenomenon is presented to students to interpret. Students then design a method to explore and collect data on the phenomenon in small groups. Next, students write their methodology and record observations. Next, an explanation with written evidence is crafted for argumentation to defend the group's reasoning. Finally, an oral argument session is held, and groups can revise their written explanations based on oral feedback. Next, the group completes a written report in alignment with the writing rubric. The students' reports are deidentified and given to two other peers in the class for the assessment using the rubric. The students' reports and completed rubrics are then given back to the students for continued revision of the written work. The final written report is turned in for a summative assessment, and an oral debrief of the inquiry activity is completed with the class.

Case Studies

Case studies are accounts of real, often puzzling or problematic situations presented to students for practice working with complex, real-world issues. Typically, a case study includes a narrative about a question or problem in need of a solution, a decision-maker and his/her perspective, data, context, and constraints. Additional supporting elements including web links to testimonies, statements, maps, videos, and so on may also be provided. Student teams or individuals can be tasked with studying the provided case materials and, from them, developing one or more potential solutions. Case studies are a favored instructional strategy among teachers because of their usefulness in promoting critical thinking through content analysis and the authentic, high-interest contexts of the cases (McClam & Woodside, 2005). Whether the assignments range from short, one-paragraph responses to fully developed group action plans, case studies represent excellent options to integrate writing into a lesson.

Digital Platforms

Finally, digital platforms are a motivational tool to enhance student literacy skills which also embody a form of twenty-first-century literacy skills known as digital literacy. The navigation of a digital platform, while motivational at times, is not enough. Students must use the platform to evaluate, analyze, and create writing products. Digital platforms provide opportunities for written peer review and ongoing content discussions. Student writing assignments can be presented as digital products in the following ways: (1) Blogs, (2) Discussion Board Posts, (3) Wikis, (4) Infographics, (5) Tutorials, (6) Digital Storytelling, (7) Audio Visual Presentations.

LEARNING TO WRITE LIKE A SCIENTIST

As with members of any other profession, scientists must produce diverse writing products for multiple, and often vastly different, audiences. Still, some writing products are distinctive to the discipline. Below are the two most universal scientific writing products that students should practice and learn.

The Lab/Field Notebook

All scientists, regardless of field, use some type of notebook for record-keeping during lab and fieldwork. These notebooks have specific qualifications, depending on the particular scientific discipline. For example, chemists and microbiologists may use carbon copy notebooks with pen entries, while field biologists may use a waterproof paper notebook and pencil or waterproof ink entries. Regardless of the scientific discipline, all notebooks have the same fundamental elements. First, notebooks are used for describing scientific methodologies or protocols. Students learning to write like scientists can use their notebooks to copy established methods or create their own. There is no universal standard of format, which makes teaching students to write in notebooks a bit easier—pick the format that will work best for you, given your learning objectives. Second, notebooks are for recording original data. As with methodologies, data can be recorded in any way that is logical given the nature of the data (e.g., tables, lists, descriptions, etc.). Third, and perhaps most importantly, notebooks are used to record original thoughts, whether questions or ideas, related to the experiment at hand. Students should feel free to express their inquiries, observations, conjectures in a penalty-free space. Science notebooks are personal as well as essential information storage documents.

The Research Report Formal Writing Lab and Research Reports

The most recognized writing product specific to science is a formal report. For students, these reports are often in the form of a lab/experiment report or scientific paper. For professional scientists, these typically take the form of published articles and agency reports. In all cases, these formal reports

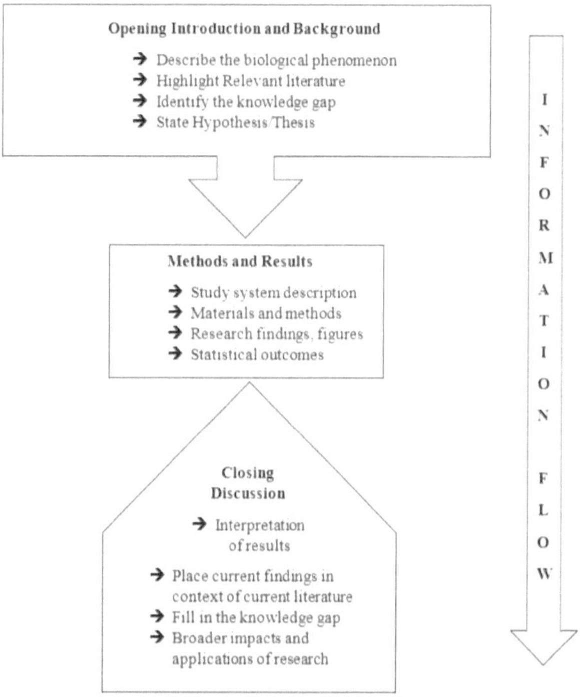

Figure 7.1 Schematic Representation of Information Flow and Standard Subsections in Scientific Reports.

are written according to a standard flow of information and text sequences not necessarily used with the same regularity in other professional fields (see figure 7.1).

Scientific reports in the biological and psychological sciences typically make use of the American Psychological Association citation style. However, the American Chemical Society is adhered to in chemistry and the American Institute of Physics style is used in physics. The writing style itself, particularly concerning voice and tense, varies by scientific discipline and can therefore utilize first or third person and either passive or active voice. It is standard to paraphrase in all scientific disciplines instead of quoting, contrary to the use of quotes in the Humanities.

SCIENCE WRITING ASSESSMENTS

The first thought for most people who hear learning and assessment in the same sentence is the dreaded TEST! True, a test is an assessment, but only one type of assessment and is usually a summative outcome representing the student's level of mastery of the learning outcomes. Teachers assess students for the following three reasons. First, teachers assess students for learning. Second, teachers assess students as they learn. And third, teachers evaluate students' level of learning.

The assessment for learning through writing in science helps teachers plan and understand how well their instructional activities assist students in learning both the science learning objectives and their progress in effectively communicating their understandings in writing. Teachers should assess student writing in science, and students should be given opportunities to self-assess their writing progress. Most of the writing in science should not be punitive but used as a formative assessment to gauge students' content knowledge and writing ability *as they learn*. The evaluation of students as they learn helps both the educator and student know if the student is on track with their progress of learning and writing in science.

The assessment of learning through science writing can be achieved by writing in any form of assessment: projects, experiments, lab reports, essays, and journals. The key to picking a summative assessment format is to ensure it allows learners to demonstrate mastery of both the learning and writing objectives. The assessment modality should be chosen based on the teacher's judgment and the learner's needs. Giving a learner choices in their assessment method to demonstrate writing and concept mastery is a way to meet the needs of diverse learners in a classroom.

Rubrics

A rubric is a qualitative assessment tool that lists the assignment's criteria and the quality of the learner's level of performance in meeting that criteria (Reddy, 2011). Rubrics are often considered the most objective way to give accurate and reliable feedback to learners regarding their writing. Rubrics can be used in the following ways to aid in science writing instruction: as a baseline assessment for students' writing ability in science, a tool for the teacher and student to use as students' progress in their writing abilities, and a summative tool to indicate a level of mastery in science writing.

Some rubrics may be generic enough to use across various writing assignments within a course because it captures most of the desired writing objectives. The general (or holistic) rubric may be a time-saver for teachers but does very little in giving specific feedback to a writer for improvement. The holistic rubric (see table 7.1) provides a single score based on the overall work assessment. In contrast, the analytical rubric provides scores for separate parts of the work, and these scores are combined in a final overall assessment score.

Rubrics can be used with a model writing sample analysis to increase students' ability to understand rubric criteria and apply the requirements to their

Table 7.1 Holistic Rubric for a Scientific Lab Report

	Developing (1)	*Average (2)*	*Proficient (3)*
Criterion	The scientific content of the report is underdeveloped and missing most of the required sections. In addition, proper writing format is not followed and references are lacking.	The scientific content of the report is partially developed and may be missing some of the required sections. The proper writing format is followed with few errors and there are some references.	The scientific content of the report is fully developed within all the required sections. In addition, the proper writing format is followed with references included.
Comments			

writing (Sitar, 2004). This can be done by giving students a model science writing sample purposely riddled with errors, not meeting the rubric criteria, for students to evaluate. Students use the rubric to perform error analysis on the writing sample and assess the writing by the standards which will be applied to their writing. Students learn the expectations of science writing through the critique and peer review of the paper of others.

In summary, holistic rubrics are beneficial when teachers need an efficient grading tool to give general writing feedback to many students. Analytical rubrics break down writing into specific criteria rated in multiple dimensions to give more pointed feedback to students. Rubric choice is dependent upon learner needs, instructional style, and classroom environment. It is important to remember that rubrics are one assessment tool. Any embedded writing-to-learn science activities can be coupled with a rubric and used as a formative or summative assessment depending on the instructional goals.

DIFFERENTIATION AND DIVERSE LEARNERS

The goal of an educator is to meet the needs of all students in their classroom, including those who are culturally and linguistically different. Instruction for culturally diverse students and students with disabilities should maintain rigor and provide students with continuous feedback.

Culturally relevant science writing curriculum means taking the writing curriculum and related literature and books and making it culturally and ethnically relatable for students of diverse backgrounds regardless of the culture and ethnicity prevalent in the book or learning resource (Toppel, 2015). Cultural responsiveness is not an added part of a unit, such as teaching the way a particular culture speaks, eats, or dresses. According to Toppel (2015), teachers address and include those of diverse backgrounds through diverse ways of communicating, thinking, and writing. Garcia and Okhidoi (2015) asserted that teachers must infuse cultural relevance in writing resources and content within their classrooms to reach diverse students. Writing is culturally relevant to someone when that person can identify with the characters, experiences, time, locations, setting, and familial and cultural references being written about. Textbooks, resources, and writing assignments should be sensitive to these attributes to ensure cultural inclusiveness.

Montelongo and Herter (2010) described the following writing strategies as beneficial to all students when learning to write in science and are particularly helpful for English Language Learners (ELLs) and students with disabilities (SWD). One, use graphic organizers to specifically outline the expository text features of problem-solution, compare-contrast, or cause-effect. Two, modify sentence completion tasks by providing students with essential vocabulary and the basic structure of science writing to use as a stem to complete their writing. Three, as available, give the students access to language translation software (free and easily accessible online) for students to explore vocabulary and translation in both their native and the English language.

Visual aids, pictures, word banks, and drawings are also valuable tools for ELLs and SWD in conjunction with peer collaboration. Writing is intertwined with the spoken word; ELL students are learning both simultaneously as they explore new discipline content. Instructional strategies must be intentionally embedded to scaffold the writing-to-learn science experiences for ELLs and SWD.

CLOSING REMARKS

On any given day we, as instructors, have choices to make about what and how we intend to engage our students so that they learn and enjoy doing so. We use technology, games, images, models, activities, and—yes—writings. Will we choose the same options every day, for every lesson? Surely not. Will we have our favorite options? Most likely. We hope that we have provided you with a valuable list of choices that you can visit, as needed, to remind yourselves of both the values of writing in the sciences and ways to use writing to help your students learn science and write like scientists. Below is an anecdote highlighting an unspoken disconnect between what we, as instructors, know to be of value for our students versus what they, themselves, think about writing in the sciences. May this story embolden you to stay firm in your commitment to using and emphasizing writing in your classrooms. Enjoy and best wishes for many happy, productive years of instruction.

VIGNETTE

At the end of my first semester of teaching at my current institution, I came across a particularly curious student comment in a postcourse evaluation. Now, let me insert here that reading course evaluations is never an easy and relaxed event. I always need to be in a particularly open yet sturdy state of mind to reap the instructive benefits of all comments, whether well considered, effusively complimentary, or scathing. The course was an introductory biology course, and the comment was, "too much writing! you're a Biology teacher, not an English teacher." Yes, I know there is a word choice error in the comment, and this is just one of many reasons why writing in science—as in all disciplines—is important. It was only at that time, after what had already been eight years of teaching, that I realized many students do not recognize the importance of and need for writing in science. How, I wonder, do they think we get jobs, communicate with each other, apply for funding, debate hypotheses, and so on? And how do they think we got to be scientists or teachers (or any science professional) in the first place? My point being, we as teachers and professionals, fundamentally understand that writing is essential. It is practically assumed and innate for us. But clearly, the fundamental nature of writing is not universally understood among our students, regardless of their ages (the student in the above scenario was a college freshman). So, our challenges in teaching students to write, think, and behave as scientists are at least twofold: one, we must convince them of the universality of good writing, and two, we must teach them the skills to recognize, create, and use it.

REFERENCES

Bandura, A. (1977). Self-efficacy: Toward a unifying theory of behavioral change. *Psychological Review, 84*(2), 191–215.

Brown, P. (2019). Explore-before-explain. *Science and Children, 56*(9), 38–43.

Clark, D. (2010). Constructivism and Instructional Design. http://www.nwlink.com/~donclark/hrd/learning/id/constructivism.html.

Dlugokienski, A., & Sampson, V. (2008). Learning to write and writing-to-learn in science: Refutational texts and analytical rubrics. *Science Scope, 32*(3), 14–19.

Elbow, P. (1973). *Writing without teachers.* Oxford University Press.

Garcia, G. A., & Okhidoi, O. (2015). Culturally relevant practices that "serve" students at a Hispanic serving institution. *Innovative Higher Education, 40*(4), 345–357.

Grant, M., & Lapp, D. (2011). Teaching science literacy. *Educational Leadership, 68*(6). ASCD. http://www.ascd.org/publications/educational-leadership/mar11/vol68/num06/Teaching-Science-Literacy.aspx.

International Literacy Association. (2017). Content area and disciplinary literacy strategies and frameworks. https://www.literacyworldwide.org/docs/default-source/where-we-stand/ila-content-area-disciplinary-literacy-strategies-frameworks.pdf?sfvrsn=e180a58e_6.

Hobson, A. (2000). Designing science literacy courses. *Journal of College Science Teaching, 30*(2), 136–137.

Longfield, J. (2009). Discrepant teaching events: Using an inquiry stance to address students' misconceptions. *International Journal of Teaching and Learning in Higher Education, 21*(2), 266–271. http://www.isetl.org/ijtlhe/pdf/IJTLHE732.pdf.

McClam, T., & Woodside, M. (2005). Using case studies: An international approach. *International Education, 34*(2), 36–45.

McLeod, G. (2016). Learning theory in Instructional Design. Learning Matters. https://www.principals.in/uploads/pdf/Instructional_Strategie/learningtheory.pdf.

McLeod, S. (2019). Constructivism as a theory for teaching and learning. Simply Psychology. https://www.simplypsychology.org/constructivism.html.

Merriam, S. B., & Caffarella, R. S. (1999). *Learning in adulthood: A comprehensive guide* (2nd ed.). San Francisco: Jossey-Bass.

Montelongo, J. A., & Herter, R. J. (2010). Using technology to support expository reading and writing in science classes. *Science Activities, 47*(3), 89–102.

National Academy of Sciences. (1996). *National Science Education Standards.* https://www.nap.edu/read/4962/chapter/1.

Reddy, M. Y. (2011). Design and development of rubrics to improve assessment outcomes. *Quality Assurance in Education, 19*(1), 84–104.

Rhem, J. (2009). Journal keeping. *The National Teaching and Learning Forum, 19*(1), 1–12.

Sampson, V., Grooms, J., & Walker, J. (2009). Argument-driven inquiry: A way to promote learning during laboratory activities. *The Science Teacher*, *76*(8), 42–47.

Singletary, A., & Sampson, V. (2011). Learning to write and writing-to-learn in science. In J. Wheeler-Toppen (Ed.), *Science the Write Way* (pp. 49–55). NSTA Press.

Sitar, C. (2004). Successful lab reports through model analysis. *Science Scope*, *28*(2), 35–38.

Toppel, K. (2015). Enhancing core reading programs with culturally responsive practices. *The Reading Teacher*, *68*(7), 552–559.

Turner, T., & Broemmel, A. (2011). 14 Writing strategies. In J. Wheeler-Toppen (Ed.), *Science the Write Way* (pp. 17–23). NSTA Press.

Chapter 8

Writing Like an Historian

Padraig Lawlor and Chantelle MacPhee

ONCE UPON A TIME IN HISTORY

When you write a story, a narrative history, you need to consider the setting, the time period, what is real, and what is fiction. You cannot set a story in eighteenth-century London, for example, and have cars on roads. With this in mind, you are about to become a myth buster, at least fictionally, but you will use the historical details you have learned in class to write your story. There have to be elements of truth and fiction in order for the story to be believable. A great story is one that is rooted in reality and merges it in a unique way into fiction. For you, the myth of William Blake warning Thomas Paine that he is about to be arrested for treason is about to become truth.

Write a narrative in which you are William Blake, the British Romantic poet who is a friend of Thomas Paine. You have learned that Thomas is about to be arrested and charged with treason, and you want to warn him and assist him in fleeing the country. Consider the following as you develop your two-page narrative.

1. How will you notify Thomas about what is planned? (Remember the time period and what is available at your disposal.)
2. How will you assist Thomas in escaping? (Consider the time period and the forms of transportation available.)
3. The tone is fear and anxiety as you try to warn him in time to escape. Make the reader feel William's fear and anxiety for his friend. Choose words that capture these emotional responses. It is your story, so feel free to decide the outcome. Perhaps, for example, he does not escape in his first attempt but something happens where you hint at a potential next chapter in the story.

4. Plan your escape by considering where Blake and Paine would be living, according to the myth, and be able to explain how Paine gets away.
5. Vary your sentences from simple to compound-complex. For example, you may wish to write something like the following: William knew he had no choice but to warn Thomas. Who could he trust? No one! How does he tell Thomas without raising suspicion? This, unfortunately, was going to take time to plan out, but time was not on his side. William needed to get Thomas out of town—quickly. Thomas's life was at stake and William's decisions here could alter the fate of history.
6. Consider your audience, the purpose of your story, and the context. Then, start writing.

As the above example tries to show, writing is a process, one that is constantly shifting as you write and learn, but writing is so much more than that. Toby Fulwiler and Art Young (1982) in their "Introduction" to *Language Connections: Writing and Reading across the Curriculum* argue that writing is meant not only to inform but also to persuade (p. x). However, in order to persuade, students must learn how to use language precisely, concisely, and with purpose. Every word matters. For students, writing about history means citing dates and trying to remember key historical figures who helped shape a nation, or a state, perhaps a province. However, writing in history is so much more. In fact, writing-to-learn is designed to shape the way in which we approach a subject and its content. We write to synthesize information, to develop a voice in the conversation that is happening in the history books. Students are not only merely memorizing dates and key figures, but they are also working toward a goal—to learn the material and how the figures and events they are studying have shaped history, a nation, and the world, and how it impacts their everyday lives.

In 1967, Canadian communication theorist Marshall McLuhan wrote his now-famous book, *Understanding Media: The Extensions of Man*, which has been reprinted many times, and titled the first chapter, "The medium is the message." This coined phrase seems particularly apropos today since technology has shifted the way in which we communicate (p. 7). While technology then was nowhere near as powerful as it is today, McLuhan's examination of cartoons, advertisements, and photos clearly aligns with the visual learning strategies we implement in today's classroom to ensure that all students learn course content. At the same time, McLuhan (1967) introduced an innovative way to tell a story—to narrate cultural, literary, social, or historical events and/or figures. His understanding of the power to communicate is important when developing classroom activities.

When coupled with the VARK learning method (visual, auditory, reading/writing, and kinesthetic), developed by Neil Fleming (1995), an interactive learning environment for all may be created. In VARK, Fleming (1995) posited that there are four ways to learn, and students and teachers in a tertiary education system, one associated with postsecondary education, use this method. However, the K–12 population could also benefit from lessons that focus on the senses because VARK enables all students to learn in the approach that best aligns with their skill set. In essence, the VARK method ensures that all students can learn in the classroom. A narrative history assignment, when delivered in Padlet or Notepad, for example, combines the VARK model with a medium designed to collaborate and engage with peers in the classroom. The senses are fully engaged as the story of historical events, people, and places is brought to life. Students do not need to memorize dates and places in history. History is no longer lecture driven when so many opportunities are available for teachers and students to write, engage, and learn.

STUDENT SAMPLE

The following student sample is one in which two middle grades education students, Allison Asher and Molly Hammond, worked as a group throughout the semester in producing their narrative histories. With their permission granted, the following is one of their narrative histories. The focus was not only on primary sources—Frank McCourt's (1996) memoir *Angela's Ashes*—but also on social and cultural history, on the creative process, and understanding the harsh reality of growing up poor in Ireland during the Depression. However, their student sample also touched on the human condition, survival of the fittest, and overcoming poverty and illness to be successful.

The purpose of the narrative history assignment was to engage students in the social and cultural history of McCourt's memoir and to explore, from his point of view, how his narrative history was constructed both in the novel and in the film of the same name: *Angela's Ashes*. The combination of the two media enabled the audience to interpret, to engage with the text itself, and to comment upon the memoir and McCourt's own revisiting of the events that transpired in his childhood. Allison and Molly used Notepad and provided a timeline, maps, and photos to develop a narrative that began a conversation around the novel itself and the social and cultural history. Molly and Allison used the Socratic method, asked questions of their peers and professors, to assess our own conceptions and understanding of Frank McCourt and the time period—the cultural and social aspects about which he was writing. In fact, Allison and Molly's group work combined two historical theorists' views on history—Arthur Marwick (2001) and Keith Jenkins (2003)—further indicating that history is not just primary sources, reiterating key dates, but a culmination of social, cultural, and political circumstances that shape a narrative, tell a story about our ancestors, whether told through a written narrative, with the assistance of Notepad or with some other educational tool, such as Padlet or Flipgrid.

INFORMATION ON CHAPTER CONTENT—THEORETICAL/SCHOLARLY SUPPORT

Arthur Marwick's *New Nature of History* (2001) and Keith Jenkins's *Re-thinking History* (2003) are two radically different views on the study of history, but an examination of both works sheds light on alternating views within the world of historical scholarship. While they are radically different, though, they are both valid ways in which to study history, but why not combine elements of both in narrating the story of our ancestors? Why do we have to choose one over the other?

British social historian Arthur Marwick (2001) is straightforward in his assessment of historical writing. For him, historical knowledge "depends on highly skilled and difficult work among the primary sources" (p. xiii). Marwick (2001) believes that professional historians use sources to remain objective and unbiased when "producing knowledge about the past" (p. xiii). To support his argument, Marwick (2001) draws upon three fundamental areas of history: knowledge, evidence, and language. Based on empiricism, the theory that all knowledge is derived from sense experience, Marwick (2001) first alludes to the process of producing historical knowledge. An important feature of this belief is an antipathy to any kind of philosophizing, such as postmodern theory. He is careful in dividing the past from written history. History is much like science, where we develop ideas through an examination of the past by means of collaborative effort. Marwick (2001) upholds his belief that through empirical study and collaboration, a historian seeks to create knowledge of the past and dismiss any preconceived biases in himself or his intended audience.

Allison and Molly's process reflects an attempt to create knowledge of the past while also avoiding biases as they learn about events, figures, and what has helped shape history. Marwick (2001), while he would agree with the collaborative effort, emphasized a one-dimensional approach to history with a focus on primary sources. Primary sources are essential to historical research, but the dismissal of unconventional historical study is restrictive. Marwick (2001) assumed that history, through the use of the archive alone, could be reconstructed. He dismissed alternate avenues for historical investigation.

History is articulated by the writer's pen. The challenge for educators is how to engage students in the task of writing about history while maintaining the integrity of primary sources.

Evidence is key to Marwick's thesis. Sources are crucial to his argument; therefore, he posited that history should strive to be methodical and precise. It is through the evidence contained in the sources that we can reconstruct the past. By merely applying theory to the historical narrative, we are doing the past a disservice. Ironically, Marwick's loathing of postmodernist theory morphed his argument into one riddled with biases and objectivity. Finally, language is portrayed as the main tool of historical communication. Essentially, Marwick (2001) argued that language was a strong interconnecting element in the study of history. It is the means to share conclusions, which are derived from the collaborative examination. He argued that precision was needed in order to avoid frivolous and objective history. The cause behind historical examination is to provide an untarnished account of past events. He posited that in order to do so, historians must remain impartial in their interpretation of the past.

Marwick (2001) strived to convince the reader that in order to reconstruct the past, the historical examination should be supported through primary analysis alone. The implication being that this method dispels biases and allows for an unblemished record of the past. What weakened his argument is his written tone and agenda-driven concepts. While Marwick's thesis certainly instigated further consideration into the dilemma, he left one with a sense of frustration.

British historiographer Keith Jenkins (2003) provided an alternative perception of how one should undertake historical analysis. *Re-thinking History* encapsulated the idea that both history and the past are separate entities. The past is something that cannot be fully revived; therefore, the information historians have at their disposal is limited. In addition to this, historians are limited due to their own biases. They are a product of the society in which they are educated. Jenkins (2003) outlined his thesis through three short chapters. First, he directly addressed the question regarding what history actually is, and how historical examination can be undertaken through a variety of means. Second, he adapted this answer to some of the issues and problems commonly debated. He argued, "although regularly posed, such issues and problems are more rarely resolved or put into context, leaving them tantalizingly open-ended/mystifying" (p. 4). Finally, he pulled together his main concepts in order to inform the reader why it is important to separate the past from written history. He reiterated how one's environment can often skew one's outlook on the past. He referred to these times as "postmodern."

Jenkins suggested that we do not run from alternative methods of historiography, but we should intellectually embrace them. Drawing upon works by Michel Foucault among others, he argued that by adopting a relative reading one can pose questions reflecting the nature of historical works. These questions can include the characteristics of the author, such as their background, and beliefs, empathy, biases, and source authenticity. The implications of this can be fruitful to our understanding of historical readings. Jenkins was very much aware of the problems associated with the study of history, and his argument was convincing. He suggested historians have been so fanatical in treating history as a science that they have underestimated the power of critical thinking through alternate means. Intriguingly, he advocated for the reader to ask why certain questions are probed in texts, while others are rejected. This system of interrogating sources should not be taken lightly, but it should be seriously scrutinized. Jenkins (2003) stated, "there is then a need for detailed historiographical studies to examine how previous and current histories have been constructed both in terms of their method and their content" (p. 82). Jenkins (2003) posed some questions on individualistic narratives of history. He consistently prodded the reader to contemplate how and why we view history just as he provoked the instructors to postulate how to deliver complex historical material to their students effectively.

Like the theoretical richness of the varied approaches to history, there also exists a rich body of literature concerning the effective teaching of history in the classroom. While the traditional lecturing model remains a popular pedagogy, novel teaching styles continue to seep into classrooms to strip away at the traditional lecture. Trepanier (2017) and Copeland (2005) stated that perhaps the most popular style involves the Socratic method. Coined after Greek philosopher Socrates, this is a system of cooperative argumentative dialogue between individuals. It is grounded on asking and responding to questions to stimulate critical thinking and to draw out ideas and underlying presuppositions. In addition to critical thinking, reasoning and logic also underscore the tenants of the approach. The aim is for students to solidify their knowledge of a particular case by thinking critically under pressure.

One further way to improve instruction is the Harkness method. Smith and Foley (2009) argued that when combined with the Socratic style, it is a potent remedy to the archaic lecture-only model. Named after Edward Harkness, the method involves an active, discussion-based learning style that requires students to take the lead and manage the class discussions. The method "flips" the traditional class model, allowing the students to learn in a way in which they are not just sitting and taking in instruction, but rather, they are required to listen, observe, analyze, verbalize, and provide visual descriptions.

THE ROLE OF THE HISTORIAN

Historians fulfill a vital role in society by acting as preservationists of the past, one that is multidimensional in nature and requires a myriad of skills. The study of History relies upon skilled historians to discover and interpret information of the past. Historians assume many important roles within society. Within academia, historians craft papers where they present their findings through research. At universities, historians often research and teach. Research allows for a greater understanding of the past, whereas teaching educates students on the historian's craft and the past itself. Historians are not just found inside universities; they educate the public through a variety of positions such as in museums and archives. History is not just about remembering dates and facts; it concerns the recovery and reconstruction of the past through means of research and investigation. Historians are concerned with the continuous, systematic narrative and research. To historians, history is an argument about what evidence should or should not mean. Despite piecing together the fundamental story of what happened, like puzzle pieces, they rarely reach a consensus on the meaning behind the narrative.

Historians are individuals who have dedicated their careers to developing skills to carry out investigations into the past. Thus, the title of "historian" can be used to describe those who have acquired graduate degrees (therefore acquiring the necessary experience and skills) in the discipline. There are many pitfalls associated with examining the past. For example, oral history poses difficulties due to unreliability and exaggeration. It is a historian's responsibility to be aware of these difficulties and to methodically overcome these problems. One solution would be to contextualize the sources with others and adapt a quantitative approach that would allow for a thorough examination.

The value of understanding the past can be seen in how the modern world works. Institutions, for example, that govern a great deal of our everyday behavior took shape hundreds (if not thousands) of years ago. Historians study the trends of past centuries, pinpointing the events that have had the greatest impact on our world. The development of historical analysis involves examination and analysis of ideas, facts, and purported facts to create coherent understandings of past events. Historical analysis is not only the study of basic concepts (such as dates and key events), but it also draws upon other fields such as English, Sociology, Psychology, Anthropology, and Philosophy, all in an effort to broaden our knowledge on a particular topic. Further, a vital component of what makes a historian is the use of historiography. This is the study of the methodology used by historians, specifically the systematic, theoretical analysis of the methods applied to History. The main body (the text) of primary documents is often key to the record. However, this can only tell so much. The author and creation date also offer valuable information relating to the document.

Historians are divided by the topic on which they focus. These concentrations often involve regions, time periods, or subfields within the discipline of history (such as social history). These divisions are often interlinked to make up a specialization. Within their area of specialization, historians pull together historical information from a wide variety of resources in an effort to "piece together the puzzle." Key to this is the dissemination and examination of primary material. These are original materials that have not been altered or distorted in any way. Examples of primary materials include artifacts, original documents, recordings, or other sources of information that were created at the time under study. Historians also use secondary material, which cite, comment on, or build upon primary sources. They are often used to supplement primary material to help understand the context of the primary material.

Historians are not just researchers; they also educate through teaching. They often instruct students at all school levels and assist in training future historians. Many historians spend their time working directly with members of the public in areas such as museums, libraries, and historical sites. These historians help inform the public as to why it is important to pursue the knowledge of the past and preserve important documents, sites, and artifacts. The accessibility of historical information is reliant upon archives to hold and preserve the sources. Many historians work in archives, organizing and making information readily available for others who need access. Others curate artifacts and artworks in museums and other sites.

STRATEGIES/TEACHING TIPS

The first tip concerns the instructor's need to build an inclusive, open classroom where different perspectives are not only tolerated but also encouraged. By its very nature, history is saturated with controversial themes and subjects. Thus, students should be able to engage with controversial material with a critical eye. This philosophy is something we have tried to make plain to our students on the first day of class. Even if history is not their favorite subject, the very process of engaging and learning in our classes will have a direct and advantageous impact on their other studies and in their future careers. Therefore, history classes simultaneously teach students the necessary skills to succeed while helping students achieve their dreams and transform their lives and the lives of those around them.

Further, the history instructor's aim is to prompt the students to engage with the world around them by showing them how their past shapes the present. History can be perceived as a dry, boring subject by a significant portion of students. We strive to show them that history is far from dull and that the significant events of the past are intricately linked with the way they lead their lives. This growing sense of connection between the past and present makes students further engage with the world around them. We seek to divorce history from an image of dusty books and lists of dates and expose it as a discipline that can make students step away from insular thinking and engage a larger world.

Reacting to the Past

Second is in regard to the development of a strategy. The traditional lecture-style approach is necessary in history classes given the sheer depth and breadth embodying many events. However, this pedagogy could be supplemented with alternative pedagogical approaches. One such method is the "Reacting to the Past" series. This centers on historical role-playing games that explore important ideas by re-creating the contexts that shaped them. Students are assigned roles that are informed by classic texts and set in historical moments of intellectual and social ferment. This learning activity helps students improve their oral communication and presentation skills. The game demands that they pay attention to their place in particular contexts. The benefits transcend the learning material in the classroom as it reminds students that verbal skills are important in everyday life. For instance, if one is tasked to sell an idea, product, or service, they must do it through both proper speech and charisma. They learn about the consequences of speech and thinking about every word they say and how others may interpret it—a lifelong skill so necessary in the workplace today.

A major benefit of the Reacting to the Past game is to encourage the quieter students to speak their minds and partake in classroom activities. Students are often shy to speak their opinions. Having students portray different characters places them in scenarios in which they can learn by actively participating. It situates the students in the mindset of individual characters in history. Moreover, it keeps them proactive with reading and learning. When students are confronted by a classmate portraying another character, it creates a unique dynamic where they must defend their position utilizing their knowledge of history, prepare their words and actions to align with their character's aims, and use effective communication skills.

Lesson Examples

The Socratic style combined with the Harkness method can create effective lessons. Dr. Lawlor once assigned readings from classic writers Herodotus and Thucydides to be read and analyzed in his Medieval Civilization class.

Subsequently, students were given a small amount of time to craft arguments highlighting which of their particular writer's interpretation of events, such as the Peloponnesian War, was the "correct" one. The activity was both fun and invigorating, but the most remarkable part was seeing the pensively quiet students gather the courage to speak their mind in the discussion. It was affirming to review this activity with the students afterward. Not only did they critically listen to their classmates' stories to develop points of argumentation later in the discussion, but also they harnessed their collective strengths to put forward a robust and reasoned case of their own at the conclusion of class. This was a "lightbulb" moment for many students, several of whom later confessed they had not considered the broader utility of history classes until that activity encouraged them to consider the varied perspectives of other people groups.

In Dr. Lawlor's and Dr. MacPhee's Irish History and Literature class, modules were designed using a variety of media, based upon Marshall McLuhan's "the medium is the message" as the foundation upon which this course was conceived. Both Dr. Lawlor, a History professor who also studied English as an undergraduate student, and Dr. MacPhee, an English professor who also studied History as an undergraduate student, decided to combine elements of storytelling in their class as a way for students to synthesize historical texts with literary interpretations. The class was a combination of History and English majors who wanted to learn about Ireland. All activities were designed with the students in mind. In fact, the historical narrative was designed to combine literary and historical elements so that students could not only interpret the history they were learning, but also interpret it from a literary and creative viewpoint. What emerged from this activity was a plethora of synthesized narratives that informed the reader about events and people from a cultural and social perspective and linked it to their own lives. By doing so, students felt they were participants in their learning and often shared their work with one another. In essence, students in this interdisciplinary course learned that music, art, literature, and history, when united, develop a narrative of the past that is engaging, interesting, and most of all, a learning experience. Perhaps Marwick (2001) would confront both of us about the potential biases of our students in constructing assignments that did so, but at the end of the day the students learned to synthesize, to tell a story that interested them about history, and to use the skills they have learned in previous English and History classes to do so.

In this way, perhaps Marwick (2001) is right in claiming that an examination of the past must be a collaborative effort in which we learn from each other, provide feedback for each other, and share in our experiences. Allison Asher and Molly Hammond discovered this in their Notepad presentation on Frank McCourt. At the same time, Jenkins's (2003) postulation that history and the past are two separate entities is clearly revealed in the narrative histories our students produced. When our students wrote their narratives, they inserted their biases, their interpretations, but they knew when they did so. They understood why they were writing what they did, whether to add elements of surprise, of conflict, or a quest that may not align with historical fact. That, in the end, is an important learning objective in itself. Marwick (2001) and Jenkins (2003) may have differing perceptions of history, but when the two main theories are juxtaposed, an interesting third option occurs—the students learn how to write a narrative, why they write what they do, how to engage a reader, how to synthesize literature and history, and they develop critical skills for the workplaces that await them upon graduation. They learned to write and wrote to learn.

REFERENCES

Copeland, M. (2005). *Socratic circles: Fostering critical and creative thinking in middle and high school*. Stenhouse Publishers.

Fleming, N. D. (1995). I'm different; not dumb. Modes of presentation (VARK) in the tertiary classroom. In A. Zelmer (Ed.), *Research and development in higher education, proceedings of the 1995 annual conference of the higher education and Research Development Society of Australasia* (pp. 308–313). HERDSA.

Fulwiler, T. & Young, A. (1982). Introduction. In T. Fulwiler & A. Young (Eds.), *Language connections: Writing and reading across the curriculum* (pp. ix–xiii). National Council of Teachers of English.

Jenkins, K. (2003). *Rethinking history*. Routledge.

Lee, T. (2005). *The Socratic method today: Student-centered and transformative teaching in political science*. Taylor and Francis.

Marwick, A. (2001). *The new nature of history*. Lyceum Books.

McCourt, F. (1996). *Angela's ashes: A memoir*. Scribner.

McLuhan, M. (1964). *Understanding media: The extensions of man*. McGraw-Hill.

Smith, L. & Foley, M. (2009). Partners in a human enterprise: Harkness teaching in the history classroom. *The History Teacher*, *42*(4), 477–496.

Chapter 9

Keeping it Real

Supporting Writers in the English/ Language Arts Classroom

Holly S. Atkins and Lisa Delgado Brown

In this chapter, we will be exploring authentic ways to teach/reinforce literacy concepts with your students. Open a social media platform, turn to an article you have saved, or simply scroll until you find one you would like to read. Let's examine what caught your attention within the selected piece. Was it the author's voice? Was it that it was interesting to you because it related to your interests somehow? That authenticity, and more importantly how to help your students connect to texts in real ways, as both readers and writers are at the core of what we will be exploring in this chapter. Authentic learning is classroom learning that mimics real-world practices. This type of learning is engaging and makes for a smoother transfer from the classroom to real-world application. Part of that is because students learn the skills within the classroom but can more easily generalize the skills into a variety of real-world settings.

VIGNETTE

As a new teacher, Matt wanted to teach his students skills that they could use immediately in the real world. He had heard about a local community center that was going to be closing due to a lack of funding and knew that many of his students and their families may be impacted by the loss. He brought the issue to his seventh-grade English/Language Arts classes and they brainstormed what they could do to help the situation. Matt turned this into a series of writing assignments. First, he had students research the community center, including how the project was originally funded and what services they provided to the community at large, and specifically to the kids at the local schools. Students also investigated other after-school community supports for kids in their area so that they could highlight why this community center was integral to the community. Students had to cite their sources and present their findings to each other in class. Next, the class had decided to make pleas to the community to bolster support for the community center. The class decided that there should be a variety of ways to reach the community, so some students created videos that could be uploaded to the web on social media platforms, some students wanted to write brief articles which could be included in local newspapers and community blogs, and some decided they would create campaigns which could be uploaded onto platforms such as *Go Fund Me*. Matt even reached out to the community center director and asked if they could come and talk to the class and hear some of the students' ideas.

The big takeaway with this type of activity is that while students are mastering core literacy skills (writing, researching, collaborating, communicating, etc.) they are doing so in an engaging way. The students in Matt's class learned about the issue itself, but they also learned that there is power in literacy and how it can be used to change their world. You can't get much more engaging or authentic than that!

Authenticity is reflected in our core beliefs about what constitutes effective writing instruction. We've organized our chapter around these core beliefs with the goal of presenting ELA teachers with foundational building blocks. We stand on the shoulders of giants and encourage our readers to take note of those giants of best writing practices whose voices are included here. Their voices and our core beliefs we hope will be your writing instruction touchstones to return to often.

BELIEF #1: OUR PERSPECTIVE ON LITERACY—READING, WRITING, TOGETHER AND SEPARATE

Teaching writing is such an important endeavor. Writing is one of the most foundational ways that we use to communicate with each other. Starting in the earliest of days, cavemen wrote in hieroglyphs on cave walls—hoping to leave messages for future ancestors. Yet, writing is a skill that may not come naturally to all of your students. It is a skill that needs explicit instruction and some core foundational understandings to be truly effective and communicative. The main goal of writing is to communicate with others. So, let's start at the beginning, but the beginning might not be as clear-cut as you think. First, we will explore the reading and writing connection.

Reading and writing are not only connected, but they are also completely intertwined. Research tells us that students who have a better understanding of what comprises good writing not only have a stronger understanding of reading but also read more throughout the upper grades (Korat & Schiff, 2005). Further, to see the most growth in our students, both reading and writing should be taught in tandem (Fitzgerald & Shanahan, 2000). In an experimental study of middle grades students (n=300), Lee and Schallert (2016) found that reading and writing skill development is reciprocal and that implementation of extensive reading as an effective intervention model was not only possible, but it was also "mutually facilitative" and benefited both reading and writing development (p. 159). Additionally, Stanovich (1986/2000) noted that the differences between good readers and poor readers not only increase over time, but also this difference accelerates as they move into higher grades. So, we need to keep encouraging our middle grades students to read to strengthen their writing abilities and facilitate maximum literacy growth as they move throughout middle grades and into their high school years.

According to the National Council of Teachers of English (NCTE, 2019) position statement regarding *The Act of Reading: Instructional Foundations and Policy Guidelines*: "effective literacy learning environments . . . include regular opportunities to learn and use various forms of oral and written language" (para. 5). While we may teach reading and writing as separate subjects, they are interwoven. When we write, our purpose is to convey understanding. That means we must think about how our words will come across to a reader. But other aspects, such as the cognitive, sociocultural, and developmental aspects, are equally as important and serve to highlight the multidimensionality of literacy (Kucer, 2014). Leu (2000) pointed out that not only is literacy dynamic, but also we are always in the process of becoming literate rather than being literate. These evolving understandings of literacy led to the idea that we should think of literacy as a plural construct, "literacies," because our understandings of what it took to be literate have evolved and broadened in the twenty-first century (New London Group (NLG), 1996). NLG developed a proposal for a "pedagogy of multiliteracies" that addressed the how, why, and what that had changed as our fundamental understandings of literacies expanded (Cope et al., 2017). Specifically, the multimodal nature of literacies became apparent as our knowledge base widened. Kress (2003) highlighted the need to extend our understanding of literacy beyond a focus on only print-based literacy, to also include other equally important modes of representations such as "gestures, speech, image, writing, 3D objects, color, music, and no doubt others" (p. 36). Multimodal literacies are texts and practices that use two or more modes of representation to convey meaning (Jewitt & Kress, 2003). Graphic novels (GNs) are an example of multimodal literacies that we will explore in this chapter.

Many of your students may not view themselves as readers and writers even though so much of what they do is centered around literacy; however, it is the context that is key. For example, when asked to write in class for an assignment, writing may be seen as boring, yet, when writing a piece of fan-fiction during their free time, writing is a fun and engaging social practice. When we think about how we can best motivate our students to become effective writers, we must first begin by exploring the communities of practice or affinity spaces in which they interact. Understanding adolescents' literate identities, how they view themselves as a reader and writer in various contexts, spaces, and the communities of practice in which they traverse, is crucial to helping them build a variety of skills and attitudes necessary to fully participate in our twenty-first-century world (Delgado Brown, 2019).

BELIEF #2: STUDENTS LEARN TO WRITE BY WRITING

Writing is a muscle—use it or lose it. Use a muscle frequently, it becomes stronger. Writing becomes stronger when it is embedded throughout the learning process (yes, in all classrooms). Steve Graham (2019) reviewed 28 studies involving over 7,000 teachers in the United States and throughout the world, asking what does writing instruction look like? His findings validate our six beliefs and what the National Commission on Writing (NCOW) reported in 2003: "Writing is a neglected skill" (Graham, 2019, p. 281). Graham's meta-analysis identified one of the many challenges teachers face in supporting the growth of student writers. NCOW put it this way: "in today's schools, writing is a prisoner of time" (NCOW, 2003, p. 20). Teachers can become stifled by a lack of adequate time within their suggested curriculum road maps to delve into writing deeply with their classes. We are encouraged to move on. We cannot steer off the path too much or we will be completely off course and not arrive at the anticipated finish in conjunction with other district teachers. So, what can we do to combat this? We have to get sneaky. While we need to adhere to those curriculum maps we have to look at ways to edge in more writing time. Feeling overwhelmed with all of my teacher "must dos," I reached out to a mentor-colleague whose words inform our perspective on time and frequency of writing opportunities: "Make everything count (at least) twice." Writing as an integral, natural part of the learning process in all content areas counts twice—connected with assessment, connected with responses to reading, connected with the acquisition of learning in note-taking, and so on.

One great gift we can give to our students is to teach them to write daily in a variety of ways. In middle and secondary settings many teachers have bell work exercises for students to work on during the passing period and first few minutes of class. They provide a short period to work on a daily review of key skills. As an ELA teacher, I often had a few prompts for students to address on their daily bell work activities. These included simple grammar exercises or an invitation to free write on a topic of their choice or in response to a given prompt. You would be surprised how much a middle schooler can write in response to a prompt like *What rules would you change in our school? Why?* As teachers having time set aside for daily writing practice reinforces the importance of writing to our students.

Freewrites are a simple writing practice centered around continuously writing for some time without stopping to revise thoughts or grammar. Using freewrites can be a great way to encourage students to get in the habit of writing and become comfortable with both the process of writing and writing fluently for different purposes (such as to inform, entertain, persuade, etc.). Writing fluency is a crucial skill we want to cultivate in the classroom so that students get more familiar with the ebbs and flows of writing. Fluent writing focuses not only on the process but also looks at the final product, ensuring the author's voice is clear and the purpose is apparent. All of us have an inner critic which is a great tool to harness later in the writing process, but with freewrites we just want to encourage them to get to the ideas. In other words, get your ideas down and critique later. While they are writing, we should be writing too. Perhaps you could display your screen to the students so that they can see you writing and editing at the same time. Seeing that thought process can help all students; however, it can be a huge support for struggling writers. As you create your own freewrite pieces, share them aloud to your students. Ask others to read theirs and then share what they learned by hearing the thoughts and musings of others. This helps develop their knowledge in such a way that the classroom becomes a series of collaborative partnerships, where peers are a continued resource for each other.

BELIEF #3: CREATING AND SUSTAINING A COMMUNITY OF WRITERS IS ESSENTIAL

Classrooms can become communities of practice if the students share membership and identity in the learning that takes place there and are united by a particular learning goal (Wenger, 1998, 2011). The importance of building a classroom community should not be underestimated. Now, how can you cultivate such a community in your classroom? In most cases it takes methodical forethought—everything from the types of activities you plan to the arrangement of desk and grouping practices should be considered when planning for community collaboration.

The first thing I would suggest is to rearrange the classroom to have the focus be on the students and strengthening their relationships. The goal should be finding a grouping that helps learners collaborate, such as a group of three or four. I always tried to find ways to build up my students by working together in flexible groups. For example, if we were working on word choice, I would craft mixed ability groups created with a mixture of students who were working on that skill. Mixed ability groups can facilitate peers working together to build critical thinking skills and extend each other's thinking (Park & Datnow, 2017). Mixed ability groups lend themselves easily to differentiation and benefit struggling learners (Lou, 2013).

One facet that needs to be cultivated is the connection, or sense of belonging, that students have within the classroom community. Adolescents' literate identities, how they see themselves as a reader or writer, are a core component of who they are as a literate learner (Beach & Ward, 2013). Students may have a different perception of themselves as a literate learner in the classroom than they do in online platforms based upon their perceptions of competence and membership in digital contexts (Delgado Brown, 2019). As teachers, we need to find out what kinds of things our students do in their free time that may impact their literate identities. There are a variety of contexts in which learning takes place outside of the school setting. In fact, Gee (2007) discussed the vast amount that students can learn from playing video games. Gee (2004) has described the importance of creating spaces where people were united by fluid participation and where they benefited from a collective intelligence. Gee was describing what has come to be known as affinity spaces.

Affinity spaces can exist in many contexts. In this way, what we really want to do is take our classroom communities to the next level, incorporating Gee's affinity spaces to transform our classroom communities into affinity spaces, where they are united by more than mere membership in a class, acknowledging that they have come together to create a shared understanding and increase their collective knowledge. In order to fully embrace this idea and transform our classrooms, we need to emphasize distributed knowledge from a wide array of sources and acknowledge a variety of participation platforms. Teachers should be learning alongside their students and should allow students opportunities to learn and engage in learning from a variety of environments and methods especially with the onset of technological applications and contexts (Gee, 2004, 2018). Viewing our classrooms as affinity spaces allows students to engage in learning, in more authentic and real ways, where they are united by shared understandings and ideas.

BELIEF #4: AUDIENCE + PURPOSE + GENRE + SPACE = ROADMAP FOR EFFECTIVE WRITING

"If you tell your students what to say and how to say it, you may never hear them, only the pale echoes of what they imagine you want them to be" (as cited in Kittle, 2008, p. 16). Donald Murray's words should give pause to all teachers of adolescents. Remembering that we teach students, not content. Remembering that these students walk into our classrooms each day wanting to be known and to be provided with a sense of autonomy and agency for making their individual voices heard. Murray's words also point to the need for authenticity. Our students must be engaged in writing for real audiences and real purposes throughout a range of genres. Writing a summary for you, or an argumentative essay for the state test does not grow writers. When student writers are invested in the self-selected topic and a self-connected purpose for writing, they are engaged and committed to getting it right—to ensure the reader gets it right, gets just what the writer wants and needs to communicate. This engagement and commitment leads to motivation to carefully draft, edit, revise, and so on and as a result, writing skills improve (Kittle, 2008). My eighth graders were drafting letters as part of their service-learning projects. They'd identified someone in a position to impact the community issue central to their self-selected projects. One day I showed students where to find the envelopes and stamps when they'd finished their letters. I was met by blank stares. Finally, Marcus spoke up asking, "We're going to send these letters for real?" and took his "finished" letter from the turn-in folder. Others followed. Clearly, the teacher as the sole audience wasn't motivating those student writers to get it right.

Authenticity in audience, purpose, and associated genre moves student writers' questions from "How long does this have to be?" to internal questions of how to get it right. Penny Kittle puts it this way, "The writing task drives revision; if the task is an assignment, the student will depend on the teacher for revision suggestions, editing, and so on, focused on what the teacher wants instead of what the writing needs" (Kittle, 2008, p. 157).

BELIEFS #5 AND #6: WRITING SHOULD BE TAUGHT, NOT JUST ASSIGNED: TEACHERS NEED TO WRITE WITH, FOR, AND IN FRONT OF THEIR STUDENTS

Our belief in the importance of modeling writing as a writer is such an integral part of our belief in the need to teach writing, not merely assign it, that we're giving ourselves permission to present these two beliefs together.

Anne Ruggles Gere refers to writing as a "specialized professional activity" for writing teachers, just as painting and singing/playing an instrument are for their colleagues in art and music (Gere, 1980). Gere's words are echoed throughout the National Writing Project's core beliefs about effective writing in K–12 schools. Teachers who write can personally understand the process of producing effective writing. They understand that all writing that becomes public involves a level of risk-taking. How can we not do what we expect our students to do almost daily: write and share in front of others? Time is one of the most precious commodities in the classroom. We carefully craft lessons that engage our students in "bell to bell" meaningful learning. As teachers, we must also maximize our time—attendance to take, emails to respond to, and all those papers stacking up waiting to be graded. It is tempting and understanding to take care of some of those tasks while students are writing. But remember that students are watching. They know about time. They know that what you do is important. So what you spend your time doing carries the stamp of importance. Reading while your students are reading says reading is important. Writing while your students are writing says writing is important. Sharing what you've written and the triumphs and challenges you experienced in the process of crafting that writing, students learn that both process and product are important. They also know that in this community of writers, we are all in the process of *becoming* and that we do so with collaboration and support.

He who learns from one who is learning, drinks from a flowing river (African proverb).

This native American proverb illustrates the teacher-student-writers process of becoming. Of vulnerability and risk-taking. Of showing, not telling.

BELIEF #7: WRITING SUPPORTS SHOULD BE CRAFTED WITH INTENTIONALITY

Working with struggling students can be facilitated by asking help and support from various specialists who are familiar with the specific needs of the students. Perhaps they have an accommodation sheet that has already been created as part of their IEP or you should have access to their latest WIDA test results. And it may not just be kids who are identified or receiving support that struggle, oftentimes the struggle may come unexpectedly. If you approach each lesson thinking that some students may struggle, then you will always be prepared to remediate as necessary. Using tools such as planning sheets and graphic organizers can help all students, but especially those that you know struggle with writing. Also, focusing upon a specific skill set within a piece may be helpful. For example, if you use the 6+1 Traits of Writing maybe in each larger piece you focus on one key element with students that are struggling. So in a given assignment all students may participate in writing, but instead of focusing on many areas, maybe these struggling students are just focusing on honing their voice. I had a Wow Word Sheet that all students had and could use when revising and editing their work. It had lists of commonly used words, such as "alot," and possible substitutions.

BELIEF #8: GRAMMAR AND MECHANICS MUST BE TAUGHT WITHIN THE CONTEXT OF STUDENTS' (AUTHENTIC) WRITING

Lauren sits at her table, arms crossed, a scowl on her face—clearly she has some opinions on how the previous night's script-reading at the local theater went. "Lauren, any thoughts?" I ask, knowing Lauren is a thirteen-year-old full of wonderful, strong thoughts. And what comes out of her mouth next are words that not only fill my English teacher's heart with joy but become a compass in my growth as a writing teacher. "Don't those actors know anything about punctuation? An ellipse is not the same as a comma or a period!"

What to do about grammar? From grammar workbooks and daily oral language to a hands-off, students will pick this up on their own approach, English educators have long struggled with how to support student writers in developing proficiency in grammar, usage, and mechanics. Constance Weaver's seminal 1996 text, *Teaching Grammar in Context*, made the bold claim that writers master the elements of grammar best within the context of their own writing. Jeff Anderson echoed this perspective nearly ten years later as he shared his own struggles as a middle grades language arts teacher. Providing his adolescent writers authentic opportunities for writing in which a compelling reason for writing is communicating to others, Anderson developed a pedagogical perspective built upon writing as thinking. "English teachers often take a right-wrong stance. I'd rather my students take a thinking stance" (2005, p. 4). When students write for real audiences and real purposes, the motivation to get it right compels these authors to attend to what they find meaningless in isolated grammar exercises.

BELIEF #9: WRITING IN DIGITAL SPACES SHOULD BE AN INTENTIONAL PART OF WRITING INSTRUCTION

In addition, students need to be taught how to write using technology. While I still find it useful to sketch ideas out on paper sometimes, I have migrated almost exclusively to using technology. I personally appreciate the ease with which we can edit and also share our work when it is on a digital platform. Not all of our students have a lot of exposure to using and writing on digital platforms. They could benefit from a quick demo providing explicit instruction on the basic features, especially if it is a platform that is new to them. My own daughters used the Google Suite in their previous schools but when they began instruction in a new school district that utilized Microsoft platforms there was a learning curve.

The kinds of practices that we want to include in our classrooms should be composed of "real-world literacy instruction for real-world literacy use" (Kucer, 2014, p. 9). In 2003, the NCOW recommended that we examine how we teach writing, calling for many changes, including more time devoted to writing instruction. Unfortunately, in 2021, eighteen years later, we are still dealing with issues surrounding time, "in today's schools, writing is a prisoner of time" (NCOW, 2003, p. 20). In order to mediate this, the literacy activities that we bring into our classrooms should be as authentic as possible. Literacy instruction should not be just a set of instructional practices or strategies, but a dynamic framework that includes a variety of pedagogical tools that are fluid, situated in a variety of contexts, and includes overt instruction (Cope et al., 2017; NLG, 1996).

BELIEF #10: WRITING FLOATS ON A SEA OF TALK

Prompt presented. Timer set. I sit at my desk with pen and paper, ready to write with my students during silent writing time. I emphasize the need for silence. I say, The goal here is to keep your pen moving across your paper for the full 5 minutes. You can begin with the prompt, but feel free to follow where your thoughts and writing lead you. We'll share afterward, but now is silent writing time. The students nod and begin writing. Then the student-to-student murmurs begin. I use eye contact, facial expression, finger to the lips to remind them that this is Silent Writing Time! I admit this scenario repeated far too many times before I came across these powerful words from James Britton (1983) that changed my writing practice: "Reading and writing float on a sea of talk" (p. 11). Well of course! Those student-to-student murmurs were prewriting activities! When I embedded time to talk before writing, quiet (mostly) and productivity soared.

Our belief is that learning itself floats on a sea of talk, and providing students oral language opportunities supports analytical thinking critical to effective writing. Authentic conversation can help students explore deep issues. This can be particularly helpful for diverse and struggling students who may need some additional time to process and work through complex issues. In the ELA classroom, we want to provide purposeful instruction that

Table 9.1 Oral Debate Overview

Grades:	*Ninth*
Activity Time: 1 week	One day to read/analyze poems. Three days for drafting/revising/editing. One day for presentation.
Standards:	*Comprehension and Collaboration* CCSS.ELA-LITERACY.SL.9-10.1 ***Initiate and participate effectively in a range of collaborative discussions (one-on-one, in groups, and teacher-led) with diverse partners on grades 9–10 topics, texts, and issues, building on others' ideas and expressing their own clearly and persuasively.*** *Presentation of Knowledge and Ideas* CCSS.ELA-LITERACY.SL.9-10.5 Make strategic use of digital media (e.g., textual, graphical, audio, visual, and interactive elements) in presentations to enhance understanding of findings, reasoning, and evidence and to add interest.
Description:	Have a class debate where students explore the pros/cons of a certain issue or have them craft a response describing their stance on an issue. Look for topics to compare, for example, exploring thematic issues such as love, oppression, or prejudice from different characters' perspectives. For example, students compared different facets of love from Shakespeare's *Romeo and Juliet* with messages in song lyrics. Answer *Is it love?* Or, *How can one come to define love?* Provide textual evidence to support the claims.

connects their talk to a collaborative task or explicitly guided instruction. By starting with talk, we acknowledge that communication is the cornerstone of literacy.

One way to incorporate oral language into the ELA classroom and build on the connection to writing is through class debates. Below is a sample one-week overview of a debate activity in a ninth-grade English classroom (see table 9.1).

PUTTING IT ALL TOGETHER IN THE ELA CLASSROOM

In this chapter, you have explored several key tenets of writing instruction. Writing should not be an afterthought, rather, it should be a core component of our ELA instruction. Students need time allotted for practicing writing, and assignments requiring deep exploration and explanation. Utilizing authentic practices help engage our students and provide opportunities for that deep exploration we need to help our students develop their voice and hone the craft of writing. There should also be consistent and purposeful use of scaffolds and accommodations for struggling writers. Finally, we need to plan for the types of digital tools we can integrate within our classrooms as a core component of writing instruction. We need to teach our students not just how to use those digital tools, but how to write in that space. This keeps our classroom instruction authentic and real.

GRAPHIC NOVEL PROJECT

What do these beliefs look like in an English/Language Arts classroom? How do they frame our daily teaching? Take a look at this one example of a graphic novel project that pulls these beliefs together.

GNs are multimodal novels that are rich in images that are paired with text, similar to comic books. GNs can provide ongoing visual support within the text that helps guide readers' comprehension. In creating graphic novels, writers must include visual and textual supports within the texts they craft. Researchers support the use of redefining and reconceptualizing literacy instruction to better prepare our twenty-first-century students to communicate through and across a variety of texts (Galvaldon-Hernandez et al., 2017). According to the NCTE, multimodal literacy instruction should become an "increasingly important component of the English/Language Arts (ELA) classroom" (NCTE, 2005, p. 1). Researchers have noted many benefits to using GNs, such as the fact that illustrations can act as a scaffold for struggling readers, attract reluctant readers, and further enhance the understandings of successful readers (Mathews, 2011). Additionally, they have been shown to scaffold comprehension (Breanna, 2013; Cohn, 2020), increase their interest in the text (Lenters, 2018), and practice fluency (Brown, 2013). GNs are not only supportive and engaging texts to read, but they can also provide an authentic writing activity for your middle grades students.

FOUNDATIONAL BELIEFS ARE ONLY THE BEGINNING

As English/Language Arts educators, we acknowledge that this chapter is far from comprehensive. Our goal was not to attempt to present ELA teachers with all they need to know about teaching writing. If your journey in reading this chapter ends with a knowledge of the critical, foundational practices needed to grow effective, engaged, motivated writers, then we consider our mission accomplished. If you're ready to continue that journey, we hope you'll use the reference section as your must-read list to continue your growth as an ELA teacher.

REFERENCES

Allen, J. K. (2016). Using enrichment clusters to address the needs of culturally and linguistically diverse learners. *Gifted Child Today, 39*(2), 84–97.

Anderson, J. (2005). *Mechanically inclined: Building grammar, usage, and style into writer's workshop.* Stenhouse.

Benson, S. (2010). "I don't know if that'd be English or not": Third space theory and literacy instruction. *Journal of Adolescent and Adult Literacy, 53*(7), 553–563.

Brenna, B. (2013). How graphic novels support reading comprehension strategy development in children. *Literacy, 47*(12), 88–94. https://doi:10.1111/j.1741-4369.2011.00655.x.

Britton, J. (1983). Writing and the story of the world. In B. M. Kroll & C. G. Wells (Eds.), *Explorations in the development of writing: Theory, research, and practice* (pp. 3–30). Wiley.

Brown, S. (2013). A blended approach to reading and writing graphic stories. *The Reading Teacher, 67*(3), 208–219. https://doi.org/10.1002/TRTR.1211.

Clark, J. S. (2013). "Your creditability could be shot": Preservice teachers' thinking about nonfiction graphic novels, curriculum decision making, and professional acceptance. *The Social Studies, 104,* 38–45.

Cohn, N. (2020). Your brain on comics: A cognitive model of visual narrative comprehension. *Topics in Cognitive Science, 12*(1), 352–386. https://doi:10.1111/tops.12421.

Cook, M. P. (2017). Now "I" see: The impact of graphic novels on reading comprehension in high school English classrooms. *Literacy Research and Instruction, 56*(1), 23–53.

Cook, M. P., & Sams, B. L. (2018). A different kind of sponsorship: The influence of graphic narrative composing on ELA pre-service teachers' perceptions of writing and literacy instruction. *Journal of Language and Literacy Education, 14*(1), 1–25.

Cope, B., Kalantzis, M., & Abrams, S. S. (2017). Multiliteracies: Meaning-making and learning in the era of digital text. In F. Serafini & E. Gee (Eds.), *Remixing multiliteracies: Theory and practice from new London to new times* (pp. 35–49). Teachers College Press.

Delgado Brown, L. (2019). New literacy memberships: Imaginative implications for 21st century literate identities. Language development and Literacy: Proceedings of the IAFOR International Conference on Education Conference Proceedings. https://papers.iafor.org/submission45083/.

Fitzgerald, J., & Shanahan, T. (2000): Reading and writing relations and their development, *Educational Psychologist, 35*(1), 39–50. https://doi.org/10.1207/S15326985EP3501_5.

Gavaldon-Hernandez, G., Gerboles-Sanchez, A., & Saez de Adana, F. (2017). Use of graphic novels with preservice teachers as a mediated learning tool. *International Journal of Social Sciences, 3*(2), 1323–1336.

Gee, J. P. (1996). *Social linguistics and literacies: Ideology in discourses* (2nd ed.). London: Taylor & Francis.

Gee, J. P. (2004). *Situated language and learning: A critique of traditional schooling*. Routledge.

Gee, J. P. (2007). *What video games have to teach us about learning and literacy* (2nd ed.). Palgrave/Macmillan.

Gee, J. P. (2018, February 26). Affinity spaces: How young people live and learn online and out of school. *Phi Delta Kappan: The Professional Journal for Educators*. https://kappanonline.org/gee-affinity-spaces-young-people-live-learn-online-school/.

Gere, A. R. (1980). Teachers as writers. *The National Writing Project Network Newsletter, 2*(2), 1–2.

Graham, S. (2019). Changing how writing is taught. *Review of Research in Education, 43*(1), 277–303. https://doi.org/10.3102/0091732X18821125.

Green, S. K., Smith, J., & Brown, E. K. (2007). Using quick writes as a classroom assessment tool: Prospects and problems. *Journal of Educational Research & Policy Studies, 7*(2), 38–52.

Hammond, H. (2010). Graphic novels and multimodal literacy: A high school study with American Born Chinese. *Bookbird, 50*(4), 2–32.

Jewitt, C., & Kress, G. R. (2003). *Multimodal literacy*. P. Lang.

Kittle, P. (2008). *Write beside them: Risk, voice, and clarity in high school writing*. Heinemann.

Korat, O., & Schiff, R. (2005). Do children who read more books know "what is good writing" better than children who read less? A comparison between grade levels and SES groups. *Journal of Literacy Research, 37*(3), 289–324.

Kress, G. R. (2003). *Literacy in the new media age*. Routledge.

Kucer, S. B. (2014). *Dimensions of literacy: A conceptual base for teaching reading and writing in school settings* (4th ed.). Routledge.

Lee, J., & Schallert, D. L. (2016). Exploring the reading-writing connection: A year-long classroom-based experimental study of middle school students developing literacy in a new language. *Reading Research Quarterly, 51*(2), 143–161. https://doi:10.1002/rrq.132.

Lenters, K. (2018). Multimodal becoming: Literacy in and beyond the classroom. *The Reading Teacher, 71*(6), 643–649. https://doi10.1002/trtr.1701.

Leu, D. (2000). Literacy and technology: Deictic consequences for literacy education in an information age. In M. L. Kamil, P. B. Mosenthal, P. D. Pearson, & R. Barr (Eds.), *Handbook of reading research* (Vol. 3) (pp. 743–770). Routledge. https://www.researchgate.net/publication/246704243.

Lou, Y. (2013). Within class grouping: Arguments, practices, and research evidence. In J. Hattie & E.M. Anderman (Eds.), *International guide to student achievement* (pp. 167–169). Routledge.

Moje E. B., Ciechanowski K. M., Kramer K., Ellis L., Carrillo R., & Collazo, T. (2004). Working toward third space in content area literacy: An examination of everyday funds of knowledge and discourse. *Reading Research Quarterly, 39*(1), 38–70. https://doi.org/10.1598/RRQ.39.1.4.

Murray, D. (1985). *A writer teaches writing*. Houghton Mifflin Harcourt.

National Commission on Writing. (2003). The neglected "R": The need for a writing revolution. https://www.vantagelearning.com/docs/myaccess/neglectedr.pdf.

National Council of Teachers of English. (2005). *Multimodal literacies: A position statement.* http://www2.ncte.org/statement/multimodalliteracies/.
National Council of Teachers of English. (2016). *Professional knowledge for the teaching of writing: A position statement.* https://ncte.org/statement/teaching-writing/.
National Council of Teachers of English. (2019). *The act of reading: Instructional foundations and policy guidelines: A position statement.* https://ncte.org/statement/the-act-of-reading/.
New London Group (1996). A pedagogy of multiliteracies: Designing social futures. *Harvard Educational Review, 66*(1), 60–92. https://www.researchgate.net/publication/265529425.
Park, V. & Datnow, A. (2017). Ability grouping and differentiated instruction in an era of data-driven decision making. *American Journal of Education, 123*(2), 281–307. https://doi10.1086/689930.
Shaughnessy, M. (1977). *Errors & expectations.* Oxford.
Stanovich, K. (1986). Matthew effects in reading: Some consequences of individual differences in the acquisition of literacy. *Reading Research Quarterly, 21*, 360–406.
Stanovich, K. E. (2000). *Progress in understanding reading: Scientific foundations and new frontiers.* Guilford.
Walsh, M. (2017). Multiliteracies, multimodality, new literacies, and . . . what do these mean for literacy education? *International Perspectives on Inclusive Education,* 11, 19–33. http://doi.org/10.1108/S1479-363620170000011002.
Weaver, C (1996). *Teaching grammar in context.* Heinemann.
Wenger-Trayner, E., & Wenger-Trayner, B. (2011). How are communities of practice different from more familiar structures like teams or task forces? Team BE. https://wenger-trayner.com/resources/how-are-communities-of-practice-different-from-more-familiar-structures-like-teams-or-task-forces/.

Index

About the Contributors

LAURA ALTFELD, PHD

Laura Altfeld is an associate professor of Biology in the Department of Mathematics and Sciences at Saint Leo University. Dr. Altfeld has a broad educational background with a BS in Marine Science from Eckerd College in St. Petersburg, FL, and both a MS and PhD in Biology from the University of South Florida in Tampa, Florida. She serves as the associate director of the Honors Program and has been instrumental in obtaining external funding to support numerous academic programming at Saint Leo, including serving as the PI of a current National Science Foundation grant that supports STEM teacher preparation.

HOLLY S. ATKINS, PHD

Holly S. Atkins earned her BA, MEd, and PhD in Curriculum and Instruction from the University of South Florida. Prior to arriving at Saint Leo University, she worked as a middle grades English/Language arts teacher and served as the codirector of the Tampa Bay Area Writing Project. She is an associate professor of Education and the chair of the Undergraduate Education Department at Saint Leo University. Her teaching focus includes the writing across the curriculum course in the Middle/Secondary program. Dr. Atkins's scholarship focuses on adolescent literacy and identity exploration, meaningful learning with technology, and writing across the content areas.

CHERYL BERRY, MED, MS

Cheryl Berry joined Saint Leo University in 2017 as an instructor of Biology and Life Sciences. Cheryl has over fifteen years of experience in science education at all levels of K–12 public and private schools as well as higher education. Cheryl received both her BS in Environmental Science and MS in Instructional Design from Saint Leo University. She also has an MEd in Curriculum and Instruction from the University of South Florida and a graduate certificate from the University of South Florida in Informal Environmental Education. Cheryl is a current doctoral candidate with the American College of Education in Curriculum and Instruction with an emphasis in STEM Leadership. She is currently a codirector of the ACES program, an NSF Scholarship Program for STEM + Ed majors, and facilitates an environmental youth summer camp at Saint Leo University. Cheryl's research interests include instructional practices that lend to increased inclusiveness of women and other underrepresented groups in STEM education.

LIN CARVER, PHD

Lin Carver joined Saint Leo University with over thirty years of experience as a teacher and administrator in K–12 schools (teacher, coach, and director) and as an adjunct professor at various universities prior to joining the Saint Leo University community in 2010. She currently serves as the director of Program Approval in the College of Education and Social Services and the program administrator for the master's in Reading Program. Her teaching responsibilities are in Graduate Studies in Education in the Reading, ESE, Instructional Leadership, and Education Doctorate programs. Her presentations, publications, and research focus on increasing student achievement through effective literacy instruction, engagement, technology, and educational interventions.

CHRISTINA CAZANAVE, MSW

Christina Cazanave is the director of Field Education and instructor of Undergraduate Social Work at Saint Leo University. She earned her masters at the University of Central Florida. Before becoming a faculty member, she worked as a social work practitioner for ten years, primarily with at-risk children and teens in the foster care and educational systems. Professor Cazanave's concentration of studies includes macro social work—community and organizational change. Her focus includes initiatives within the social work profession to combat social injustices using advocacy and public policy. She is currently the National Association of Social Workers Nature Coast Unit chair and a member of the Emerging Leaders-Scholars Initiative Cohort affiliated with the Association of Baccalaureate Social Work Program Directors. Also, Professor Cazanave trained with Citizen University as a Civic Saturday Fellow and now leads civic engagement activities within her community. Professor Cazanave's work has been presented at multiple conferences, including at National Association of Social Work—Florida Conference, Social Work Distance Learning Conference, and the Influencing Social Policy—Macro Conference.

LISA DELGADO BROWN, PHD

Lisa Delgado Brown received a BS in Special Education, MA in Instructional Psychology and Technology, and a PhD in Instructional Leadership and Academic Curriculum, with a concentration in Reading/Literacy Education from the University of Oklahoma. Dr. Delgado Brown is an experienced educator with a demonstrated history of working in higher education and P–12 schools. Prior to her time in higher education, she served as a special education teacher, reading specialist, and literacy coach at public and private schools in Florida and Oklahoma. Dr. Delgado Brown specializes in the impact of language and literacy development on student learning, multimodal literacy development, and the use of technology to motivate and engage literacy learners. Her current research is exploring the impact of hybrid teaching on perceived K–12 student learning.

CARRIE FALLON-JOHNSON, MS

Carrie Fallon-Johnson earned her BS Ed and MS Ed in Literacy Education from the State University of New York at Fredonia. She has been teaching and leading at Pasco County Schools in Florida since 2005—primary through middle grades. Mrs. Fallon-Johnson has been a designer and facilitator of professional development in the areas of literacy and technology applications for elementary and secondary classrooms.

NAKITA GILLESPIE, MA

Nakita Gillespie earned her BA and MA in Elementary Education from the University of South Florida. She is currently an adjunct instructor at Saint

Leo University, helping to prepare the next generation of educators. Prior to joining the Saint Leo team as an instructor, she served as a codirector of the Teacher Technology Summer Institute while working in the role of learning design coach at Sand Pine Elementary School in Pasco County, FL. Her career began as a K–5 teacher in Hillsborough County and Pasco County school districts. These combined experiences have allowed her to pursue her passion of supporting teachers in transforming their classrooms through the meaningful use of technology in education.

CAROLYN E. GRAHAM, BA

Carolyn E. Graham earned her BA in English and a Minor in Early Childhood Development from Ashford University in Clinton, Iowa. She has been serving in the educational field since 2003. Her educational experience varies from Elementary Education to Secondary as well as ESE Support to Advanced Placement. She has been at Pasco County Schools in Florida since 2013 where she currently serves as a learning design coach with a strong focus on Literacy across content areas.

KIM HIGDON, PHD

Kim Higdon earned her undergraduate degree at the University of Texas, her MA in Teaching from the University of Puget Sound, and her PhD in Adult, Professional and Community Development. Currently, she is a new teacher support specialist in Round Rock ISD and is an adjunct at Saint Leo University and Texas State University. Prior to that, Kim has served as director of Reading Intervention in the South Bronx and associate professor of Education at Saint Leo University. In her thirty years as an educator, she has taught Pre-Kindergarten–eighth grade around the United States and overseas. Her passions are literacy, technology integration, and urban education.

PADRAIG LAWLOR, PHD

Dr. Padraig Lawlor is an assistant professor of History at Saint Leo University, having earned his PhD in European History at Purdue University. He also holds an MPhil in Early Modern History from Trinity College Dublin; a H Dip in Irish History from Maynooth University, and a BA (History; English) from Maynooth University. Dr. Lawlor teaches a wide array of courses on European and World History, and he has published articles and reviews in venues such as the *Journal of Political Theology*, *Seventeenth-Century News*, *H-Albion Journal*, *History Journal*, and *Capital & Class Journal*.

CHANTELLE MACPHEE, PHD

Chantelle MacPhee earned her BA from the University of Prince Edward Island, her MA from the University of Western Ontario, and her PhD from the University of Glasgow in Scotland. She has taught for twenty-eight years in four countries and has extensive experience in teaching writing as well as her area of specialization in Shakespeare and the Long Eighteenth Century, particularly poetry. She is an associate professor in the Department of Language Studies and the Arts, and she serves the faculty as the chair as well as the director of the Quality Enhancement Plan—Read! Write! Transform! Dr. MacPhee has published and presented both nationally and internationally on writing, Shakespeare, Blake, and the English Romantics.

LAUREN PANTOJA, MA

Lauren Pantoja is a learning design coach at Chasco Middle School in Pasco County, Florida, where she supports teachers in technology and literacy in all contents. She earned a master's from Webster University which she has used during her more than thirty years as a K–12 educator and coach. She also designs and teaches courses for Pasco County School District to support teachers and works as an adjunct instructor at Saint Leo University preparing future literacy teachers and coaches. These experiences provide the foundation which has resulted in her recognition as Florida Literacy Coach of the Year.

EBONY PEREZ, PHD, MSW

Ebony Perez currently serves as assistant professor of Undergraduate Social Work and department chair at Saint Leo University. Dr. Perez has over fifteen years of experience in Social Work practice and has held various roles, including behavioral specialist, research associate, inpatient psychiatric social worker, and pediatric ICU social worker. Her research agenda seeks to understand the nuances and complexities of the role of educators in preparing future practitioners for antiracist and antioppressive praxis. Dr. Perez has presented her work at numerous national and international conferences focusing on empowering marginalized communities in academic spaces.

CHRISTINE PICOT, PHD

Christine Picot is an associate professor in the College of Education and Social Services at Saint Leo University. She earned her PhD from the University of South Florida in Curriculum and Instruction with a specialization in Childhood Education Literacy Studies and a cognate in Elementary Mathematics Education. Her research interests include disciplinary literacy with a focus on academic vocabulary and mathematics instruction. This disciplinary literacy focus has led to the development of numerous publications, conference presentations, global work, and professional development. Her work with preservice and in-service teachers includes coaching and mentoring in cross-curricular connections for teaching and learning.

CANDACE ROBERTS, PHD

Candace Roberts is the director of the Center for Teaching and Learning Excellence and a professor of Education at Saint Leo University. She earned her BA in English from Emory University, and her MEd and PhD in Curriculum and Instruction in English Education from the University of South Florida. She began her career as a middle and high school English teacher. Her research interests include brain-based learning, writing pedagogy, and the integration of technology into effective instruction. Dr. Roberts has conducted more than hundred scholarly presentations and has published more than twenty articles, chapters, and papers.

www.ingramcontent.com/pod-product-compliance
Lightning Source LLC
Chambersburg PA
CBHW020741230426
43665CB00009B/517